The Classic ACs

The Classic ACs
Two Litre to Cobra

A collector's guide
by John Mclellan

MOTOR RACING PUBLICATIONS LTD
32 Devonshire Road, Chiswick, London W4 2HD, England

ISBN 0 900549 98 X
First published 1985

Photosetting by Tek-Art Ltd, West Wickham, Kent
Printed in Great Britain by The Garden City Press Ltd,
Letchworth, Hertfordshire SG6 1JS

Contents

Introduction

At intervals during the motor car's first century there have appeared vehicles of such fascination that not only have they become prized collectors' items, they have also been accepted as symbols of the eras in which they first appeared: the Bugatti Type 35, the MG Midget TC, the Ferrari 250GT – and the AC Cobra 427.

As a result there has been a flood of books and articles about the thunderous 7-litre Cobra and its marginally more restrained elder sister, the 4.7-litre Cobra 289. But despite their glamour and the excitement they can generate even 20 years on from their brief racing heyday, the Cobra story is only one chapter in the 80-year history of AC Cars, a small, individualistic, specialist car manufacturer. Run since 1930 by two generations of the Hurlock family, the company has had its seasons of glory and its brushes with disaster.

AC has survived. In itself that is no small achievement. The world has not been kind to specialist car builders in the past 15 years. There must have been occasions in the late 1970s when the beleaguered Derek Hurlock must have wondered why he still battled on. But battle he did and now he has the satisfaction of knowing that even if his own company has withdrawn from sports car manufacture, there are two separate companies building high performance vehicles bearing the honoured AC marque symbol.

This is less paradoxical than it appears. By 1967 it appeared to AC Cars that no very substantial market existed for the 427 or 289 Cobra roadsters. They were most probably correct. To sell the roadster they needed the marketing muscle of Shelby American backed by Ford, and that had been whisked away. The 428 was a different matter. They could see a market in Europe for this kind of long-legged, luxuriously equipped Grand Tourer. It was then a question of whether the production quality problems could be overcome. When yet more onerous Type Approval requirements appeared on the horizon, AC decided the big V8 cars were not a viable proposition. The AC 428 ceased production in 1973.

As one of the last of the unregulated, pre-Nader muscle-cars, the Cobra quickly gained a cult following. Since they are very cheap to build and the price of secondhand examples had leapt skywards, by the mid-1970s a whole industry was devoted to recreating Cobras from wrecked cars, on occasion retaining little more than the chassis identification plate. One of the most meticulous of these craftsmen was Brian Angliss. He moved carefully from reconstructing wrecks to building complete cars from scratch, following the methods and dimensions of AC Cars and gaining the confidence of Derek Hurlock. The next step was to update the car without changing its character and it was in this form that the Autokraft AC Mk IV was first seen in public at London's Motorfair in autumn 1982.

The second car to carry the AC badge in 1985 is the ME3000. Eric Broadley designed the Lola GT which was developed into the Ford GT40, the mid-engined projectile which supplanted the Cobra in Ford's affections. He also designed the Lola T70, which must have been the inspiration for the Diablo mid-engined coupe which AC took up and first exhibited as the ME3000 at the London Motor Show in 1973. To productionize the excellent basic concept and put it through the horrendously costly Type Approval procedures stretched AC's resources to the very limits.

As they moved, very slowly, into production, the world economy slid into a deep recession. AC Cars had relied on building invalid tricycles for the British National Health Service to cover their overheads, but these contracts were at an end. What looked like a sensible decision to diversify into commercial vehicles was hit by the recession. AC continued to build and sell the ME3000, but in minute quantity. It was an attractive package at £11,300 in standard form. There was a sunroof, electrically operated windows, tinted glass, radio and a choice of cloth or leather trim. The engine was supplied only in standard tune, but specialist Robin Rew could supply a useful turbo installation and upgrade the suspension.

A number of would-be entrepreneurs showed an interest in the car and finally, in early 1984, it was decided to hand over the ME3000 to Kirkby Hogarth, a Scottish-based company run by David McDonald, which had impressed Derek Hurlock and AC

Cars' management with its backing, expertise and enthusiasm.

In their report to the Stock Exchange, AC's directors said, 'The company has agreed terms to dispose of its manufacturing rights and interest in the ME3000 sports car to Kirkby Hogarth Limited to whom it will licence the right to use the AC trade mark and the name AC.

'To continue manufacture of the ME3000 would have required within the next few months a considerable investment in stocks coupled with the necessity for design changes arising from forthcoming National Type Approval legislation. The board did not consider such investment could be economically justified.'

Kirkby Hogarth became AC Cars (Scotland) Ltd. During 1984 the production facilities for the coupe were transferred to the new factory at Hillington, Glasgow. By early 1985 some production models were ready for delivery to new owners. Just as important, work was going on to produce the Mk II version, which will incorporate some much needed improvements to the basically sound design. It is likely that some interesting engine options will soon become available. All who enjoy the high performance car must wish the two new companies at opposite ends of the Kingdom good luck in the struggles which surely lie ahead.

Acknowledgements

All those who have written about and photographed the AC car down the years, the members of the AC Owners' Club and the Shelby American Automobile Club, Ford Motor Company, AC Cars, National Motor Museum, Autokraft.

Particular thanks to Barrie Bird, Brian Gilbart-Smith, Derek Hurlock, Keith Judd, Jock Henderson, Graham Murrell, Rodney Leach, Brian Angliss, David Hescroff, John Atkins and Barry Thorne. Finally, I gratefully acknowledge the expertise of my publisher John Blunsden and editor Ray Hutton.

JOHN McLELLAN

Abingdon, January 1985

The ME3000, production of which has now been transferred to Scotland, is one of two contrasting designs – the other is the Cobra-derived Mk IV – carrying the AC name on into the late 1980s.

7

The Pedigree – Ace, Cobra and 428

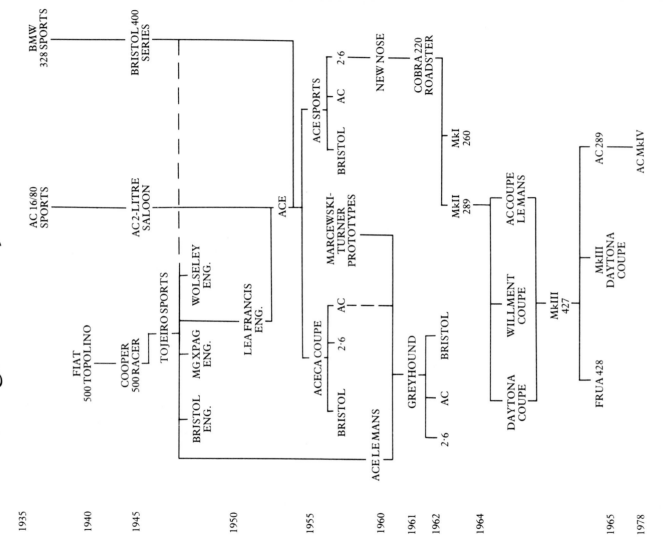

CHAPTER 1

Ancestors and parentage

From Sociable to 16/90

In 1902 a prosperous London master butcher joined forces with an inventive young engineer to build a four-cylinder 20hp touring car for display at the 1903 Crystal Palace Motor Show. Designer John Weller hoped to race the machine that bore his name, but although John Portwine's butcher shops provided funds enough to build the car and exhibit at the show, that was as far as it went. Instead, in 1904, they launched a more modest project, a tradesman's tri-car. With two wheels at front and one aft, it was driven by a thumping 5hp single-cylinder engine powering the rear wheel via a two-speed epicyclic transmission and chain. There was a capacious trunk at the front and the rider perched over the rear wheel. It was robust and well designed and by the end of 1907 the Sociable had grown from it, with a single seat for the passenger to replace the goods trunk. There was nothing very sociable about the arrangement, but the following year saw the driver alongside his passenger down at the front.

The two entrepreneurs coined Autocarrier for their goods carrier. When the Sociable became popular they adopted the AC initials for it. Their company name remained Autocarrier until November 1922, when it was changed to AC Cars Limited on the departure of the two original promoters, dislodged by the redoubtable Selwyn Francis Edge.

The Sociable was a doughty contender in the long-distance reliability trials which so forced the pace of British car evolution in the early years. It was succeeded in 1913 by a four-wheeled AC cyclecar with a neat monobloc 10hp four-cylinder side-valve engine, transverse front and quarter-elliptic rear springs. It was good for 45mph – respectable indeed in those days, with a comfortable two-seater body to carry.

Weller and Portwine both enjoyed competition and the former schemed out a sporting version with the three-speed transmission in unit with the worm-drive back axle. A skimpy, polished aluminium body helped keep overall weight below the 10cwt limit of the internationally-recognized Cyclecar category. This pretty device's career was cut short by the Great War of 1914-18 but an 11.9hp Anzani-powered sports derivative was offered soon after the Armistice. Although meant to be a stopgap, the Anzani AC was to be the company's main profit earner in the 1920s.

The luxury car market beckoned enticingly to many motor manufacturers in those first happy months of peace. It was the sensible way to go for smaller companies lacking the knowledge and capital resources to venture into the choppy waters of the mass market. There need be no unseemly price comparisons with your competitors, for who could place any real value on breeding and quality? What was charged for the product could bear little resemblance to what it cost to build. Portwine and Weller decided there was a market for a small, refined, high-performance car and to give it that essential extra ingredient, Weller set to work to produce the first small high-performance six-cylinder automobile engine.

The engine which resulted – and the ambitious record-breaking and racing programme on which they had embarked – cost so much that Weller and Portwine were constrained to seek further capital. They were unwary enough to bring S.F. Edge into their company; he became a director in February 1921. By October 1922 they were out of it, leaving Edge in command and with an attractive range of 1,500cc and 2,000cc four-and six-

cylinder cars to promote.

When Weller's reign as chief designer at the Thames Ditton factory on the southern outskirts of London ended, he left his successors two main legacies. The first was the six-cylinder engine. With 65 x 100mm bore and stroke it was a long-stroke powerplant that took none too kindly to very high revolutions, but it was scientifically designed and light. It was to be developed from the original 40bhp of 1919 to some 105bhp by the time it went out of production a record-breaking 43 years later, in 1962. The second legacy might be called 'Weller's revenge'. It was his three-speed transaxle. The unit was clever and logical for a 20bhp cyclecar, acceptable for a 40bhp 'four', but by the late 1920s had helped to generate considerable customer resistance to Edge's 2-litre Light Sixes, by then producing 56bhp and even more in Sports guise.

From 1919 to 1925 the company was a considerable force in the competition world, becoming the first team to break international 1½-litre class records at over 100mph and to cover 100 miles in the hour. In the hands of drivers of the calibre of Hawker, Joyce, Davis, Don and many others, the sleek little Weller-designed racers with their ingenious exposed axle-shaft

rear transaxles and smoothly-contoured polished aluminium bodies found success in races at Brooklands, hill-climbs, sprints and record-breaking runs from Shelsley Walsh to Boulogne and the Montlhéry track in France. Altogether AC broke 21 1,500cc class records and 19 in the 2,000cc class.

AC used three types of engine in these endeavours. The Anzani side-valve 'four', which accepted a measure of tuning and was supplied in 40bhp guise in the delightful 12/40 Sports available from 1921; the special four-cylinder 16-valve single-overhead-camshaft Weller racing engine evolved for the 200 Miles race in 1921; and the similar ohc production six-cylinder of 2 litres, used for a couple of notable endurance runs at Montlhéry track in the mid-1920s. Edge celebrated these events with the Montlhéry Six Sports, an impressive 80mph vehicle with the mandatory light-alloy pointed-tail body. Although handicapped by its three-speed transmission, the Six Sports was given quite effective four-wheel brakes (the 12/40 had rear-wheel brakes only) and by the time mounting debts forced Edge's company into voluntary liquidation in 1929, 66bhp was being put out by the engine in three-carburettor form and with a fifth main bearing to give more peace of mind at higher engine revolutions.

AC Cars were taken over by William Hurlock Junior, a South London company run by William Hurlock and his brother Charles. More interested in road haulage and spares factoring than car making, the brothers initially purchased the AC factory and its Thames Ditton site as a truck depot and bodybuilding shop. There was still a busy and profitable AC service depot there and they allowed that to continue to look after the considerable numbers of touring four- and six-cylinder AC cars by then in use. Throughout the company's history AC owners have been a loyal crew and the service manager gladly passed on to his new directors the heartfelt inquiries of owners anxious to exchange their old AC for a new one of not too dissimilar specification. From 1930 a trickle of new cars was built to order using parts discovered in the factory stores. Will Hurlock took for his personal use a Light Magna saloon, one of the last built with the Weller transmission. By 1932, as the stock of major components began to run out, it was time to decide whether or not to continue with car manufacturing.

The Hurlocks' 1930s ACs were good-looking cars. This is the author's 1933 sports four-seater with 16/66 engine.

Will Hurlock was nobody's fool. His grandfather had been Mayor of St Albans, and his father had continued the family tradition of tailoring, with a business in the South London suburbs. Born in 1890, Will launched himself in business while still less than 16 with the sale of his father's motorcycle. By his 20th birthday in 1910 he and younger brother Charles were trading as William Hurlock Junior with their own Motor House premises, selling everything automotive from spares and oils to secondhand cars.

Adaptable and quick-thinking, the brothers flourished through the 1920s. They bought and sold cars, trucks and parts. There was a busy car hire offshoot with a fleet including 'The most beautiful vehicle for hire in the whole world', a 1913 Rolls-Royce Silver Ghost landaulet, (10 guineas per day including 100 miles, further mileage at one shilling and sixpence a mile). A speciality was to recondition ex-War Department trucks for resale. They had premises in Tulse Hill, Denmark Hill and Effra Road bursting at the seams with stocks being processed, and when by 1930 a commercial bodybuilding offshoot needed more space, they were directed to the spacious and then largely empty AC factory in High Street, Thames Ditton.

Having become a motor manufacturer almost by accident, Will Hurlock brought to this business the same keenly cost-conscious approach that had served him so well in the hard world of motor transport. If neither Will nor Charles had any great leaning towards motoring sport both were experienced, even enthusiastic drivers. Will owned Glevering Hall in Suffolk and commuted at weekends in Rolls-Royce, Chrysler, Daimler and Packard cars. He had no sentimental attachment to the controversial three-speed transmission in his Light Magna saloon, but clearly realized that in its 56bhp 15.9hp RAC-rating engine, now fully developed, smooth, reliable and with tooling costs written-off in the Edge management's collapse, he had an invaluable asset. He despatched AC service manager G.R.H. Simpson to Coventry and gave him a tiny budget with instructions to find suitable axles, a gearbox with four speeds in it and ancillaries to permit a more conventional AC to be built.

The company returned to full-time manufacturing in time for the 1933 Motor Show at London's Olympia. Their marketing policy was sound. Although the engine was AC's own, all other mechanical parts, including the chassis-frame, were now bought in from specialist makers of good reputation. Elliot and Bishop supplied the steering gear, rear axles were by ENV, the four-speed manual or pre-selector gearboxes were by ENV or later Moss Gear and were assembled in unit with the engine. Body frames were built of ash and panelled in-house by AC or by

The 1935-36 16/80 short-chassis sports was one of the most handsome of its time. This car was owned by the author for a period; it had a considerable record in trials in the 1930s.

The 2-4-6 coupe could take up to six people if the rear dickey seat was used, hence its name. This beauty belongs to Bernard Driver and is still used for long-distance touring.

outside suppliers, but designs were to the company's own requirements, and all were trimmed and cellulosed to the highest standards in their High Street works.

By the mid-1930s the company had chalked out its territory. They permitted none of the complications in specification that had brought so many British makers to disaster. There was just the one engine and a single chassis in any given year; the wheelbase was shortened for the 16/80 short-chassis Competition Model in 1935 and some wide-chassis cars were also built using standard components. They were priced firmly in the middle category, above MG, Riley and Triumph, just above SS Jaguar, but below Alvis, Aston Martin or Bentley. On their stand at each London Motor Show they showed a range of mouth-watering drophead coupes, fixed-head coupes and saloons, all set off by the delectable sports tourers with their elegantly flared wings and comfortably fitted-out cockpits. They called themselves the Savile Row of Motordom, the implication being that if you were content with an SS or Triumph you had an off-the-peg job, the motoring version of a Burton or Fifty Shilling Tailors suit. The AC, on the other hand, was as personal to its owner as a Purdey sporting gun.

It was a neat trick and AC pulled it off by refusing to budge from the basic policy of standardized body and chassis components, while being prepared to vary detail specifications to the greatest possible degree. Everything was negotiable; rear axle ratios, instruments, engine tune (saloons could cheerfully be supplied with even the Arnott supercharged 16/90 engine first seen on the sporting models), gear ratios, spare wheel number and location. Provided that the basic structure was not altered, seats, leathers, fabrics and colours were totally open to the purchaser's choice at a modest supplement for each alteration. Consequently every AC was different from its sister.

No other manufacturer operating on such a small scale could offer anything like the choice and survive. AC only managed it because by the late 1930s they were becoming major sub-contractors to the British aircraft industry and the War Office as re-armament got under way. The specialist car industry in Britain was highly conservative in the 1930s. As 1940 approached they were outpaced technically by the volume producers such as Vauxhall and Morris with small family saloons of modern unitary construction and by the yet more enterprising designs from marques such as Lancia and Citroen on the Continent. With their beam axles, ash-framed bodies and separate chassis-frames, firms like AC would have been in deep trouble in a few seasons, but the matter was never tested. With the outbreak of the Second World War in 1939, car building ceased for six years or more and the world was very different when peace returned in 1945.

CHAPTER 2

The six-cylinder engine

A masterpiece of simplicity

Seen for the first time at the Motor Show at Olympia in 1919, the AC Six was based on aero-engine principles and in particular on the practice of the Napier company, not far away from AC in West London. The Napier 40/50 six-cylinder car engine of 1919 was a smaller, simpler aero engine. The AC Six was a smaller, simpler 40/50. Whether there really was a connection, whether S.F. Edge, with a foot in both doors, had a say in it, is only conjecture. In 1928 he induced journalist Edgar Duffield to claim that in October 1919 Edge 'set their (AC's) engineers to . . . producing a car which would behave like his 45 and 60hp six-cylinder cars'.

Weller's AC engine was a masterpiece of simplicity. The six separate cylinder liners were set into an aluminium casing open at the top, extended below to the centre-line of the crankshaft. There was a crossflow cast-iron cylinder head with two slightly inclined valves to each cylinder operated by rockers from a single overhead camshaft. Each combustion chamber was fully machined. Long cylinder head studs reaching right through the block clamped the whole edifice together. Four good large main bearings were provided and end location for the crank was by double thrust bearings at the front. Connecting rods were of 60-ton steel, heat-treated. Aluminium Ricardo slipper pistons were used. Weller's biggest headache was the camshaft drive. First he tried an offset worm drive with vertical shaft at the back of the engine, but like others before and since, found it costly to make, noisy in operation and difficult to lubricate. He turned to a simple inverted-tooth chain drive with clever spring-steel slipper tensioners of his own devising to prevent the very long chain from thrashing about.

This brilliant notion transformed his engine, making it easy to manufacture and undemanding in service, even when used at revolutions almost double the modest 2,750rpm he first intended. 'This device,' declared *Automobile Engineer* in 1926 of the Weller tensioner, 'is simple, crude, but highly effective.' There was also an excellent pressure lubrication system from a submerged pump in the sump. Less clever was the attempt to run without a crankshaft torsional damper. The crankshaft was certainly massive enough. Said AC's catalogue in 1919, 'every care has been taken to eliminate whip and there are no periods within the speed range of the engine'. In service, Edge found owners certainly complained about vibration periods, but he was equal to the occasion. 'You may explain that it is a power roar,' he told his staff.

Shown at Olympia in 1923 in chain-driven camshaft form, it was slow to go into full production. By October 1926 it had an additional bearing by the flywheel and there were H-section duralamin connecting rods with light cast-iron pistons, adopted to reduce noisy slap found in the earlier slipper pistons. Still producing 40bhp at 3,000rpm, the 'six' had a 5.25:1 compression ratio. The rare Sports unit had a 6:1 cr and gave 66bhp at 4,000rpm. After 1927 a flywheel mounted on rubber rings was provided to reduce crankshaft periodic vibrations. Three SU carburettors in the soon-to-be-classic AC layout appeared on a few specially prepared engines between 1927 and 1929. By 1930, 56bhp at 4,000rpm was the standard output. By 1933, roller cam followers were used and the connecting rods were made from steel again. During 1934-35 a much more effective flywheel damper was introduced in which the two

The exhaust side of the AC Six engine in early 1930s form, with the tough ENV four-speed gearbox in unit.

The carburettor side of a slightly later (1937) engine, this time with the long-lived Moss synchromesh gearbox.

The bottom end of an early Two Litre engine showing the bolts and rubber bushes of the split flywheel, which acted as a torsional damper.

halves of the wheel were connected by six bolts surrounded by rubber mouldings. The camshaft drive was then by multi-link conventional chain.

Light alloy pistons re-appeared in the 1930s and E.H. Sidney's eccentric-base camshaft made its substantial contribution to reducing the noise level of the valve-gear. It was never really ever improved upon. Standard UMB series engines gave up to 60bhp with a 6.5:1 compression ratio. UBS units, some with tulip valves and 'sports' connecting rods, gave up to 80bhp and there was a supercharged engine of 90bhp. Lubrication was steadily improved.

By 1940, the AC Six was a fine engine indeed. Crankshaft vibration was not quite cured, but hardly intruded. The old-fashioned die-cast white-metal main bearings were tolerant of long periods of high revolutions except when blown and driven far and fast. Cylinder head temperatures could be higher than desirable on long, hot Continental journeys. There would be a corrosion problem with the cylinder block long years ahead.

AC service and later sales manager Jock Henderson has recounted that during the 1939-45 war, E.H. Sidney, then works director, decreed that the old white-metal bearings be replaced with bronze shells, white-metal lined. A new water distribution system and more flexible engine mounting system using two forward feet on Silentbloc bushes was to be introduced. The latter was instead of the single trunnion attached to the front chassis cross-member. An engine built to these specifications was completed early in 1946. It had an aluminium alloy block of improved specification against corrosion. It was an improvement on earlier alloys, without entirely solving the problem. The water pump was relocated low on the crankcase, where it could still be driven by a vee-belt from a pulley on the crankshaft nose. Water flow was revised, the cooled liquid from the radiator passing from the pump to the jacket and thence upward to the head and back to the radiator. In deference to low-grade Pool petrol, the compression ratio was held at 6.5:1, at which 74bhp was generated. Larger inlet valves

The bottom end of a later series AC engine, this example showing the torsional vibration damper on the nose of the crankshaft and a solid flywheel.

were adopted. As before, the dynamo and distributor were rotated by a skew gear-driven cross-shaft towards the rear of the crankcase.

In its 1946-47 form the AC engine was an excellent example of logical, unforced development of a basically sound original concept. With its largely unchanged outlines and familiar triple SU carburettors it might be thought that little had altered within, but that was not the case. Just about the only item that would still have been interchangeable with that found on one of the early engines would have been the cylinder head gasket. The

The AC six-cylinder engine as used in the Ace and Aceca. The water pump was moved to the side of the block in 1946, and there is a rev-counter drive point just below the distributor. Handsome manifolds and downpipes helped the breathing of this engine. The dynamo has been moved to the front of the engine, a blanking plate covering the place where it would have been located if the driver's footbox and pedal installation had permitted.

crankshaft was no longer the massive Vickers-built effort of early days, but the more slender Laystall type introduced in the mid-1930s, lighter yet stiffer than the older shaft and less prone to vibration. Pistons, rocker-shafts, valves and guides, and certainly the lubrication system had been given due attention.

Even the carburettors on this engine were improved. With the bodywork planned for the postwar car, sparking plug access would have been made more difficult if the balance pipes connecting the inlet stubs had not been moved and a new balance pipe underneath them was provided. At the same time a thermostatically-controlled carburettor was fitted to give more certain cold-starting in overseas countries, for exports were to be of crucial importance if car manufacturer was to continue in the early postwar period.

CHAPTER 3

The Two Litre

A conservative revival

Like other prudent concerns, AC had given some time during the closing stages of the Second World War to think about their products in the postwar years. The late 1940s were an austere period. Raw materials allocated to the motor industry were, in theory, only available to those vehicle builders which were exporting their products. The era of cheap skilled labour had gone. Yet it was clear that in the postwar world a sizeable slice of the population had the means to buy the kind of slightly better product the AC company was so well versed in providing.

It was more than two years after the Victory before the new AC appeared, but in its well equipped, sober convervatism it was well judged and very suitable for the new conditions.

For the 1940 season, the company had introduced a new touring car in three- and five-seater form. Based, as previous ACs had been since 1933, on a Standard chassis, it possessed rather more supple suspension than other examples of the marque. Only a few were built before the war intervened to give time for reflection. This new model had certainly offered a more comfortable ride, but in achieving that, the nimbleness and responsive steering that made the AC a rewarding mount for the keen driver had somehow disappeared. The 1940 AC was really too bland. It was discarded and in 1945 work was put in hand to modernize the chassis that had served so well from 1934 to 1939.

As in 1930, the continuing excellence of the engine, now a quarter of a century old, was a major asset. It showed its age in one feature alone: its 100mm stroke, for when John Weller sketched it out back in 1918 it was thought desirable to keep bores to a minimum to reduce the annual tax, calculated on a formula which ignored stroke dimensions. The designer was also at pains to provide top gear flexibility and pulling power over a wide speed range, characteristics more readily found in an engine with a long stroke.

The chassis chosen for production in 1947 would have looked fairly conservative a decade earlier. Like the engine that it was going to carry, it was essentially a prewar design improved in a number of important points of detail.

Its main frame was of channel-section steel, stiffened with box sections and a central cruciform. The long side members passed over the front axle and swept down under the rear axle. Like all chassis of this type, it was neither strong as a beam nor resistant to twisting loads, so it was just as well that it was decided to retain beam axles front and rear rather than the independent front suspension slowly gaining acceptance amongst British quality car makers. Half-elliptic springs were used front and rear, those at the front sliding in robust trunnions at their rear end instead of the swinging shackles still to be seen on the back springs. Certainly it was old-fashioned, but it was well executed.

Prewar long-wheelbase saloon and drophead four-seaters had been prone to uncertain handling at higher speeds when fully laden; between 1936 to 1940 the engine had been nudged gently forwards to rectify weight distribution. By virtue of a new outline to the sump, the postwar chassis was able to accept an engine well forward and yet clear of the beam axle on full bump. Although the wheelbase was still a modest 9ft 9in, it was now possible to locate all the car's occupants within it, making handling nicely balanced under all conditions. Finally, an up-to-date Girling hydro-mechanical braking system was fitted.

The first prototype Two Litre had a rear-hinged bonnet and it differed externally in detail from production cars. It is pictured outside Turk's boatyard on the Thames, near Kingston.

Another view of the prototype Two Litre saloon alongside the Thames, the rear number-plate indicating that it was to be launched as a 1947 model.

The prototype car's interior was very stark, with a bench seat and leathercloth covering. The pull-up handbrake was typical of the period.

Drums were 12in diameter with hydraulic activation for the front brake shoes, mechanical for the rear. The handbrake was one of those infamous umbrella handle items, sticking up from the floor by the gearbox. It seems that only the brakes called for development work; the front ones were felt to be too fierce and the balance was adjusted before production started in earnest.

The prewar friction dampers were replaced by Woodhead telescopics and Girling piston types at front and rear. Steel disc wheels of 17in diameter replaced the prewar centre-lock wires.

On to this simple but excellent quality chassis AC loaded a spacious coachbuilt five-seater saloon body. The frames were built in the High Street Works and taken off to an outside contractor to be panelled. With its faired headlamps, deeply helmeted wings and mild vee windscreen the body was vaguely modern in outline yet harked backed to immediately prewar styles, particularly the Lagonda V12 saloon. Mindful of the

An early Two Litre outside the premises of the marque's Edinburgh distributor. The direction indicators have been moved to behind the side windows, but the windscreen is still as on the prototype.

AC's machine shop at Thames Ditton, turning out components from castings sent down from suppliers in the Midlands.

soaring cost of labour, the company adopted a new policy. The old Savile Row approach was no more. Instead the five-seater saloon was to be the main product and only modest alterations to specification would be permitted. Circumstances conspired to blur this policy eventually and there were to be open versions and shooting brakes before production ceased.

The very first Two Litre, as the model was dubbed, was kitted out with one of the drophead bodies left over from earlier days. This prototype went on the road in 1945 and was followed by the first saloon in 1946. This car differed only in detail from the production models, the most notable visual changes being in the treatment of the front windscreen frame and the provision of detachable wheel spats on the rear wings. The bonnet was a spring-loaded alligator affair and was intended to swing upwards given a tug on the lever which formed part of the AC badge on the radiator cowling. A couple of cars at least were made to these specifications and although they were quite good-looking, well-mannered vehicles, it was felt they were rather spartan even for that austere period. Cox tubular framed seats were of single bench type at the front with divided backs and the doors were lined in absolutely plain leather with a deep cubby hole low at the front. By the time of the first postwar London Motor Show at Earls Court in 1948 a traditional interior with acceptably pleated leather, separate seats, and more careful attention to detail was included.

In those days, the weekly journal testers were a forgiving set. When, at last, *The Autocar* was confronted with an AC saloon for test, they ruminated on the role of the specialist makers, 'catering for the needs of those people who want a car that is different'. It was not, said *The Autocar* sternly, simply that the car was produced merely to be different, 'but rather that it possesses particular qualities that suit the requirements of certain people', and these people purchased the same make of car year after year. Whilst on the one hand they did not want to see the beloved vehicle changed out of all recognition, on the other they did not want to buy an old-fashioned-looking new car. 'The AC company is just such a firm, rich in tradition.'

Testing a Two Litre two-door saloon in 1949, *The Autocar* felt that although the ride was not harsh, there was some motion transmitted to occupants on bad surfaces. There was compensation, though, in its capacity to corner or stop smartly

Framing-up Two Litre saloon bodies in an aura of unhurried craftsmanship.

There was plenty of leather and varnished woodwork in the production saloon. The cord to the rear window blind is visible. The steering wheel was adjustable for both rake and reach.

without fuss or tyre howl. They found steering geared for quick response 'pleasantly light' at low speeds or in country lanes. Straight-line stability was of the hands-off variety, but without sacrifice of 'very reassuring response to unexpected emergencies'.

The testers liked the airy interior and good all-round vision, the deep front seats and adjustable steering column. They were less certain about ventilation on a warm day, regarding the degree of warmth finding its way into the car to be a serious shortcoming.

The company had to be very cost-conscious as the 1940s drew to a close, for it was essential to keep below £1,000 for the Two Litre, to avoid a punitive doubling of Purchase Tax. They managed it for some time, offering the saloon at just £982 (plus £295 tax). This, of course, meant none of the beguiling variations which once enticed purchasers. They still managed to fit a rear window blind and there were good quality Smiths instruments with a speedometer inclined to read on the slow side. 'The leather trim', said *The Autocar*, 'is of the first grade over soft Dunlopillo upholstery . . . quiet but effective use is

23

Two Litre saloon frames taking shape in the main assembly shop at Thames Ditton.

Body frames to the left, cars moving towards completion in the centre, and body mounting on the right. Car building was a leisurely business at AC in the 1940s.

A Two Litre on the 1949 Monte Carlo Rally. This AC model did not shine in international events, being driven largely by amateur crews more intent on a winter break than on serious competition.

The Two Litre drophead was a pleasing car and one or two examples have survived. Only a small number of Two Litres were made with left-hand drive.

Another left-hand-drive drophead, or possibly it is the same 1948-49 example shown in the previous picture. The hood was exactly the same as those used on prewar four-seater AC dropheads.

made of polished woodwork for the instrument board.' There was a fully equipped tool-kit in a fitted tray in the boot-lid.

Modifications to this model were few. The bonnet was converted to side opening with a central hinge and a single budget lock controlled by an antique removable carriage key on each side. During 1950, from car EL1307, tubular telescopic rear dampers were used and with car 1318 opening rear quarter-lights were installed. From EL1403 the tyre size went up to 6.70 section from the original 5.50, wheel diameter going down to 16in. In 1952, at UMB 1802 W, a modern Metalastik crankshaft torsion vibration damper was installed on the nose of the crank – possibly the single most important innovation.

Those who follow through the journals the adventures of modern road-testers know that in the space of a year or two their response to existing cars is changed radically as newer, perhaps better, competitors are brought out. Between 1947 and 1952, testers of *The Autocar* became if anything more enthusiastic about the Two Litre: 'The general riding qualities of the AC are very good and although the suspension is firm, it cannot be called harsh under normal conditions.' They liked the still high-geared steering, '. . . very responsive to small steering wheel movements'. There, was, though, some kickback and some rear axle hop on poor surfaces. But considering its individuality, performance and reliability, they thought the AC, 'a very

Again an open Two Litre with left-hand drive, this time with cabriolet bodywork. The side lamp mounting indicates that it was built before 1950.

At one period there was a Purchase Tax advantage in having your AC built as an estate car, but the end result was usually as deplorable as this effort by a provincial builder, probably in 1948.

The Buckland tourer is today an undervalued classic with a lively performance. This example is owned by J.P. Wilkinson and is very original in specification.

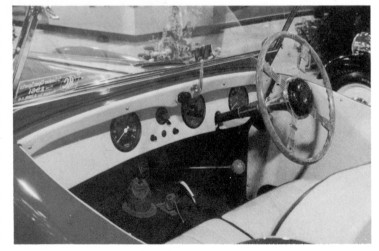

A Buckland seen at Earls Court and sporting a divided bench seat and a tachometer. It was promoted as a five-seater open sports car.

satisfactory car that will continue to have a faithful following'.

The saloon had by then been in production for five years. The eager demand for anything postwar was beginning to be satisfied. Newer, more exciting competitors were appearing. Also, the price had drifted up.

In 1948 its opposition had come from the Riley 2½-litre at £880 basic price, Armstrong Siddeley Typhoon Sportsman's Saloon (£975), Bristol 401 (£1,525), Healey saloon (£1,750) and Jaguar 2½-litre (£852). In such company it occupied a comfortable middle ground, both in price and performance. Four years later there was a different situation. As tested in September 1952 it cost £1,214 plus £675 tax, a total of £1,889. Jaguar's Mk V undercut it handsomely, as did the Riley 2½-litre. There was a new generation of high-performance cars represented by the XK120 and Aston Martin DB2 which, although they were in no way competitors to the AC, helped to make it seem old-school indeed. By then the Sunbeam-Talbot

90, much improved and with substantial rally success behind it, was a real contender in the market at £820 for the saloon. Rover had the 75 with fashionable full-width body at £865.

In 1949 AC had announced the five-seater Sports Tourer on the standard Two Litre chassis. Built by the Buckland Body Works, it inevitably became known as the Buckland, and in 1951 cost £1,098. There was a Mk 1 version in which the door was carried through at waist level. Subsequent Mk 2 versions had the traditional cutaway door with a more convenient lifting flap to the sidescreens for signalling. With a wide body structurally similar to the saloon's, large front seats with adjustable backrests, sidescreens and hood intended to make the tourer as snug in bad weather as a saloon, and a luggage boot, the Buckland was no lightweight. Tested by *Motor Sport* in 1952, a well-used version belonging to Ernie Bailey, who ran Buckland Body, proved to be capable of 86mph at its maximum permitted engine speed of 4,500rpm and did 60mph at 3,000rpm. It was found to transmit some up and down movement on uneven roads and quick negotiation of a double bend at speed resulted in some roll oversteer. The 'vintage'

During an AC Owners' Club sprint at Goodwood, Sandeman-Craik's Buckland demonstrates its steadiness and lack of roll when being cornered hard.

An impressive line-up in the service department and delivery bay at Thames Ditton around 1950.

Derek Hurlock competing with the Two Litre demonstrator on an RAC Rally. The windscreen demisters are still a useful extra on these cars when they are used in wintry conditions, although the four rear bonnet louvres were supposed to help to keep the screen clear.

characteristics of the Buckland were noted: there was some scuttle shake on very bad surfaces, but the steering was quick and with strong castor action.

Other variations of the Two Litre included shooting brakes or estate cars built by provincial coachbuilders to qualify as commercial vehicles, either to benefit from a petrol allocation in the rationing days or to avoid paying Purchase Tax. Several pleasing dropheads were built using the prewar hood framework, still available from two suppliers, Cox and Widney. An early essay was a most attractive cabriolet in which the side windows and the rail over the door were retained.

Well before the arrival of the Ace roadster in autumn 1953, demand for the Two Litre was falling. Eventually it was offered only to 'special order', AC now fulfilling that role – of supplier to customers who wished to have a new example of a rather outdated automobile – on which *The Autocar* had pondered so long before. To try to broaden the model's appeal, during 1953 a four-door version was put in hand, and it was one of these which was the last Two Litre to leave Thames Ditton in 1958.

The introduction of the Ace and Aceca in 1953 and 1954 led

The four-door version of the saloon, which was offered towards the end of the Two Litre's production life, is now a considerable rarity.

A three-quarter rear view of the slightly battle-scarred four-door model, revealing the narrowness of the rear door and the swivelling quarter-light fitted behind it.

to major improvements in AC engine specifications and the later Two Litres were also beneficiaries. Some were given Ace instruments, and it is possible that one car had a higher ratio back axle installed. When called on to fit replacement engines in the 1950s and 1960s the factory were in the habit of popping in the current-series unit, sometimes to the mystification of the owner, who found himself with an unexpectedly lively saloon as a result.

AC did not support either racing or rallying during the Two Litre saloon's lifespan. There seems little point in dwelling on the few minor successes of private owners. Only on one occasion did the car compete on level terms with its peers in the hands of a determined and skilled racing driver and that was in the Production Touring Car race at the *Daily Express* meeting at Silverstone in 1952. Young Jim Mayers, up-and-coming driver with the Monkey Stable, specialists in giant-killing MG Midgets, took one of the square-rigged old saloons – a secondhand car it was said, with 40,000 miles on it – and recorded a rousing 2min 34sec time in practice on the Grand Prix circuit. He was third fastest in the 1,500-2,000cc class behind Crook and Buckley in Bristols (2sec and 1sec faster, respectively), ahead of larger-engined Rileys and Sunbeam-Talbots.

Entered by J.K. Malcolmson, the AC proved equal to the task on race day. Mayers and Buckley had a fine old battle for second in class. Mayers finally took it by a second after averaging 66.87mph for 16 laps. He was just behind two of the Rileys; apart from Buckley, he led a Sunbeam-Talbot 90 and two Jowett Javelins over the line. Said *Autocourse*: 'The efforts of Jim Mayers with his 2-litre AC saloon – which if the makers will forgive us, one does not expect to see winning a private battle with a car like the Bristol – were most inspiring.'

CHAPTER 4

The Ace and Aceca

A winning hand from Tojeiro

In autumn 1953, practically overnight, staid old AC Cars Limited transformed itself. The company gave up building worthy but old-fashioned cars calculated to appeal to tweedy middle-class owners based in the Home Counties or The Shires – the sort celebrated by John Betjeman in his poetry. Instead they introduced an advanced, glamorous, sleek, sports-racing car, one of the most exciting products of a brilliant epoch. To understand how this came about it is necessary to glance back at two high-performance cars which went into production back in 1936.

One was AC's own 16/80 Competition Model, a short-chassis two-seater on traditional English sports car lines. With its channel-section chassis, half-elliptic-sprung beam axles fore and aft, and Thames Ditton's own 80bhp engine, it weighed about a ton. It was well-equipped, comfortable and capable of close to 90mph. In the hands of private owners it achieved some success in British sporting trials and rallies and notched up an occasional class victory in Continental events.

The second was the German BMW 328, also fitted with a 2-litre six-cylinder high-efficiency engine and producing about 80bhp. Energetically campaigned in international events by the factory, it built an enviable reputation very rapidly. Imported examples made the British domestic product seem pretty antique, for there was a neat tubular chassis and well-executed transverse-leaf independent front suspension under the BMW's mildly aerodynamic body. With a weight of less than 16cwt, it was accelerative and nimble. Between them, the two mid-1930s roadsters were to provide the power for the Ace during its 10-year career and become an important influence in chassis and

suspension design.

In the aftermath of the Second World War the rights to the fine BMW engine were vested by the victors in the Bristol Aeroplane Company, who put it into production in updated form in their own range of high-performance 2-litre cars. It found its way, too, into Frazer Nashes and into the lightweight Formula 2 cars of the Cooper Car Company which burst on the scene to such effect at Goodwood circuit in early 1952 and brought Mike Hawthorn into the public's eye.

In 1950, John Tojeiro had decided there was a better way to go racing than with the lightweight-bodied MG TA he was using. There was throughout Britain a wealth of short racing circuits, mostly airfield based. Smooth and level, they quickly bred a new kind of sports-racer. Tojeiro's approach was fairly typical. Since the only engines he could afford were not particularly powerful production units any new chassis needed to be light, offer exceptional cornering power and be capable of ensuring that what power existed was fed directly on to the road. He built simple H-shaped frames of 3in 16-gauge T45 alloy steel joined in the middle by a same-sized tubular cross-member and at the ends by 12-gauge fabricated boxes to serve as mountings for the fully independent suspension. Several chassis were built and raced.

Like the BMW 328 and the Formula 2 Cooper-Bristol, the Tojeiro had transverse leaf springs above 3/8in tubular fabricated wishbones and rack-and-pinion steering. The big innovation was that instead of a beam rear axle, there was a similar transverse leaf and wishbone rear end. Tojeiro used Morris hubs, Morris Minor rack-and-pinion steering, Turner

cast-alloy road wheels, ENV hypoid rear axle and Alfin finned lightweight brake drums.

By 1952, Cliff Davis had acquired one of these chassis and installed in it a fairly standard Bristol 2-litre engine, well back in the frame. His car had a robust hoop at scuttle level, another just behind the driver. A taut framework of tubes and drilled angle irons carried a light aluminium bodyshell, built by Bill Rich and Eddie Gray in Hammersmith, but based on the outline of the Superleggera Touring roadster for the 1949 Le Mans-winning Ferrari 122.

Davis, an experienced and forceful club driver, had a very successful 1953 season with his Tojeiro special, winning the season-long Brooklands Trophy series with the Bristol-engined car and the very similar MG-engined machine which he also raced.

Motor engineer Vin Davison built his own Tojeiro, using a 2½-litre Lea Francis-cum-Connaught engine and once again it was clad with a Ferrari 'Barchetta' type body. Ernie Bailey of Buckland knew that Charles Hurlock and his nephew Derek, son of William, were anxiously considering which way the

family business should go and it was clear the company had neither the capital resources nor design talent to create a saloon successor to the Two Litre which could compare with the new models streaming out of other manufacturers' factories. Not only was the Tojeiro a redoubtable competitor in five-lap sprint races, it also had real stamina, demonstrated by ninth place taken by Cliff Davis in the BARC Nine Hours race at Goodwood after a fire due to an unfastened fuel filler cap and time lost when a wheel was damaged at the chicane.

Davison's car was demonstrated to Charles and Derek Hurlock, works director E.H. Sidney and engineering designer Z.T. Marcewski by Cliff Davis. Derek Hurlock recalls its performance was enough to 'horrify' Marcewski, but they were impressed by the fact that here was the basis of a race-bred fast touring car. Racing had wrung out many of the bugs. The structure was easy to reproduce and would cost less than their existing production. Although the Bristol engine used by Davis was more powerful than AC's old unit – 220bhp per ton was claimed for that Tojeiro – the 80bhp that Thames Ditton knew was on tap would give performance enough if weight could be

The rear suspension of the very first Ace chassis, as seen at the 1953 Earls Court Show. Note the polished Alfin brake drum, aluminium backplate and fabricated upright.

The original ultra-light wishbones which formed part of the rear suspension of the 1953 Ace.

kept fairly near the 10½ cwt of the Tojeiro. It was summer 1953. If they moved quickly they could make quite a splash with the two-seater at the London Motor Show in the autumn.

The AC management took a deep breath. They bought Tojeiro LER 371 and hired Vin Davison to come with it as a development engineer. Much was to be done if AC were to transform a stark sports-racer into the kind of fast, comfortable and expensive roadster they had in mind. But AC knew that a huge new market for high-performance cars was waiting to be exploited in USA and on the Continent. They wanted a slice of it.

Frenzied work through the rest of the summer saw AC Cars at Earls Court with two specimens of what they now called the Ace alongside one of the trusty old saloons. Neither of the new exhibits represented the Ace in its true production guise. The Tojeiro had lost its cast wheels and sported chromed wires displaying the drilled Alfin brake drums. A tall, flat windscreen and neat hood with rigid Perspex sliding sidescreens was

The other end of the same chassis revealing the standard Two Litre radiator and the rear-mounted rack-and-pinion steering gear.

provided and the cockpit was fully trimmed. There was no time to do more.

Beside the now road-equipped Tojeiro Ace was the first AC-built Ace chassis, no. AE01 (UPJ 75). At this juncture it still had rack-and-pinion steering, mounted on light-alloy blocks aft of the front cross-member. Main chassis tube thickness had gone up to 14 swg. The front chassis cross-member itself was a stiffer structure than before. The Galley radiator with integral oil cooler of the Tojeiro-Bristol was replaced by a lowered Two Litre saloon matrix by Marston. Suspension wishbones front and rear were still the elegant and simple fabrications of the Tojeiro. To the 16in centre-lock wire wheels were fitted 5.50 Dunlop Road Speed Tyres. The light-alloy backplates of the Girling brakes were highly polished, as were the deeply finned Alfin brake drums.

The AC engine was still designated UMB as it had been on the saloons. It was installed well back in the frame to give an 18 per cent rearward bias to the weight distribution. The dynamo was installed at the front of the engine and driven by vee-belt, as was the water pump. Since the driver sat alongside the gearbox, his

The original Ace chassis from the front, showing the sturdy cross-member linking the lower suspension arms, and the fabricated uprights which connect these with the transverse leaf spring.

legs reaching forward past the bell-housing, there was no need for a remote-control gear lever to the Moss synchromesh gearbox. At the rear the fabricated cross-member doubled as oil-tight casing for the ENV hypoid bevel differential assembly with its 3.64:1 ratio. Sturdy universal-jointed Hardy Spicer drive-shafts drove through fabricated suspension uprights. All suspension pivots were of bronze with hardened steel pins. Armstrong telescopic dampers were fitted.

Although the engines used in the first two Aces – that is the Tojeiro and AE01 – were said to produce 85bhp, they differed from earlier versions only in having a 7.5:1 compression ratio and possibly some attention to the already fully-machined and near-hemispherical combustion chambers. Like previous engines from the High Street Works, these units spent eight hours running on an electric motor followed by a day and a half

under their own power, with snap output reading and a final check at 4,500rpm being made. Exit of exhaust gases was smoothed by the handsome six-branch manifold feeding smoothly into twin tail-pipes. These Ace engines were the smoothest yet, but still AC were unwilling to countenance more than 4,500rpm and at that speed the car was geared to do 96mph. In their undeveloped form these first Aces probably needed some help from wind or gradient to reach a genuine 100mph.

The 1953 London Motor Show was one of the most exciting of the series. It was labelled the 'Hundred Miles An Hour Show'. There were some two dozen different models capable of 'the ton'; they ranged from Allard and Armstrong Siddeley to Triumph and Jaguar of England, Alfa Romeo to Lancia from Italy, and Chrysler to Packard from the USA. British makers showed a mouth-watering selection of sporting machines that 20 years later were to become the backbone of the classic car movement; Austin-Healey Hundred, Triumph TR2, Jaguar XK, Aston Martin DB2-4. But desirable through these were – and they were the products of an industry at the height of its strength and confidence – in mechanical layout they offered little advance on that clever BMW 328 of 17 years before. Discounting the curious swinging-arm arrangement found on the Lagonda, only the Ace provided a convincing independent rear suspension system amongst British-built automobiles. Add to that the sturdy tubular chassis, the light-alloy bodyshell supported, Superleggera-style, on a network of steel tubes, and AC Cars had a basic design which led onward from the BMW and headed towards the thunderous Cobras.

Observers have called the Ace, 'chaste, elegant, utterly unostentatious', or, 'of Italianate simplicity'. In all honesty the Tojeiro prototype was not all of these things, but when in the winter of 1953-54 its lines were revised to place the headlamps at the height required by international regulations and provide a modicum of boot space, it became surely the most handsome British roadster of its day, a match for the Alfa Romeo Giulietta Sprint or for Ferraris by Touring. The Ace was never cheap –

A later AC-powered Ace show chassis, still with aluminium alloy backplates, but with stiffened suspension wishbones.

The Tojeiro design as transformed for the 1953 Earls Court Show. The hood and sidescreens were to survive largely unchanged well into Cobra production, but the perforated brake drums were not to be retained for the Ace.

the careful work which went into it ensured that – but it was beautiful and it was unique.

Charles and Derek Hurlock wasted no time getting the Ace into competition. After the Motor Show the Tojeiro, now registered as an AC Ace and sporting the registration number TPL 792, went through the RAC's *Daily Express* Rally with the ill-fated David Blakeley and Cliff Davis as crew. It was also road tested briefly by John Bolster for *Autosport*. He was enthusiastic, praising the car's adaptability. The well-chosen gear ratios gave exceptional acceleration, 'about 10½secs, 0 to 60mph'. He was encouraged by the AC people to ignore the 4,500rpm limit rpm and used 5,000rpm, finding the old 'six' 'dead smooth' all the way. Bolster saved his greatest praise for roadholding and suspension: 'Something the normal driver of a mass-produced saloon could not imagine in his wildest dreams'.

At a basic £915 plus tax, the Ace was priced well above its UK-built opposition, but significantly below more costly products from Porsche, Alfa Romeo or Lancia. In 1954, the Austin-Healey Hundred was £750 and the Triumph TR2 with overdrive £635. Larger specialist cars included the Jaguar XK-series – astonishing value at £1,130 – and the Aston Martin DB2- 4 at £1,850. Bolster's comment, 'with a well streamlined all-enveloping body of great beauty and typical AC finish . . . there should be a long waiting list for this 100mph car', was perhaps optimistic, but AC were to show that, as in the 1920s and 1930s, in the 1950s there was a steady demand for a performance car which offered that essential edge in handling, roadholding, finish and equipment even if it was no faster than lesser machines.

Experience with TPL 792 during the winter of 1953 and the following spring underlined the need for more power to turn the Ace into a convincing 100mph performer. The Tojeiro rack-and-pinion steering, despite giving delightfully responsive handling, was deficient in aspects of its geometry. As Jock Henderson, for so many years an AC cars stalwart as service manager and later as sales manager, observed, if the nose of the

The well-finished Ace interior with a cranked gear lever to the Moss gearbox and a fully adjustable steering wheel. The 'capped gas pipe' handbrake lever on the transmission tunnel was of the racing fly-off type.

The carpeted floor, the uncovered spare wheel and the round rear lights mark this as a very early Ace.

car was pushed down firmly the front wheels pointed gently at each other. Private owners who have experimented subsequently discovered that it is not a simple matter to provide acceptable geometry with rack-and-pinion gear on an Ace. Instead the factory used Bishop cam gear with a long transverse link and a pair of track rods pivoting on a central idler arm behind the front cross-member. It gave the turning circle of about 36ft with two turns of the steering wheel. With rigid mounts for the steering box to the chassis, little of the original feel was lost.

The AC-built show chassis was completed to close to the final specification and Ace production was well under way by late winter 1954. As UPJ 75 this prototype was to have a long and

honourable – if incident-filled – career and still exists today. Although AC were not claiming more power from the old engine, by the time *The Motor* had UPJ 75 for a full Continental test late in the year it was capable of a 0 to 60mph time of 11.4sec, and achieved a 103mph mean top speed, despite being, at 16½cwt, half a hundredweight heavier than TPL 792. During this 1,000 mile test, fuel consumption was 25.2mpg overall, hinting at efficiency despite the car's tall windscreen.

As was to happen throughout the Ace's life, the report emphasized its exclusivity. In an age when quantity-made standard products offered good quality at low prices it was, 'truly refreshing to sample a specialist car . . . which backs up its high performance with handling qualities markedly superior to

40

This left-hand-drive Ace sports the USA-type bumpers, long boot-lid and luggage rack and the early circular rear lights are fitted.

those of any lower-priced sports car which we have handled'. It recorded the best 0-80mph acceleration of any postwar car of under 2½-litres that *The Motor* had tested. This excellent performance on test was due not only to the exceptional traction provided by the independent rear suspension, but in part to the Michelin X radial-ply tyres which were used.

AC had planned from the beginning to provide the necessary equipment to enable the Ace to compete in international events. The overseas debut was in the 1954 Alpine Rally, when a works-supported three-car team went through well enough for a brand-new model, but without any awards. The team was AE26 (VPA 99), AE28 (VPA 999) and AE01 (UPJ 75). Drawing on the experience of this first major rally, AC drew up a fairly complete

list of competition goodies including duplicated coils, petrol lines and pumps, battery and petrol tank stoneguards, by-pass oil filter, and a nose cowl to reduce the air intake area. With this item the Ace's top speed was now a useful 106.5mph. Rooting through ENV's parts list, AC also offered a choice of rear axle ratios: 3.37, 4.3, 4.55, 4.88 or 5.11:1.

Once the struggle to put the Ace into production was over, it was time to think about the coupe that had been planned from the outset. At first it had been thought possible simply to provide some sort of hardtop for the Ace and leave it at that, but extended testing, especially with VPL 442, led them to conclude the end product would be too harsh, too noisy and probably too hot for comfort. There was a pause for further thought before

The first Ace to be built by the works was given the registration number UPJ 75, and is seen here after the 1955 Tulip Rally, when it won the 2-litre class driven by Gott and Moore. The Mercedes-Benz 300SL alongside it had been shared by Tak and Niemoller, the outright winners.

another long, busy summer resulted in a *Gran Turismo* coupe of acceptable refinement and even higher potential maximum speed than the Ace. It was unveiled at Earls Court in autumn 1954.

The name Aceca was revived for this delectable vehicle, making a link with the drophead coupe which had won the Monte Carlo Rally in 1926. Although the single blue prototype was based on Ace chassis AE56, there were to be so many differences a separate number sequence was allocated, beginning at AE499. Major alterations were made to the rear end of the chassis. The differential assembly was now flexibly mounted within a sub-frame attached to the chassis by three Metalastic bushes. To retain the main frame's stiffness, the tube wall thickness was 12 swg. A 3in tube was welded across between the side members just in front of the differential mounts.

A perforated sheet-steel channel was at the very rear of the main frame. To accommodate the extra weight of the coupe body the rear transverse leaf spring was stiffened. At $40^{3}/_{8}$in, it was longer than the 39in Ace spring and with two leaves $1/_{4}$in thick, four $7/_{32}$in and one $5/_{16}$in thick, rather more stiff. Free camber at the rear wheels was $5^{1}/_{2}$in, against the 5in of the Ace. Weight distribution was a traditional 46:54, front, rear.

By 1954, AC Cars had built up a considerable expertise in glass-fibre moulding and to insulate the occupants from the noise and fumes of the engine compartment the Aceca received a light but strong bulkhead moulding. There were more glass-fibre mouldings around the wheelarches. For the outer body a light-alloy skin was wrapped round a tubular sub-structure, although now there were square tubes to provide the essential strength across the windscreen and over the doors. The doors were framed in timber, as was the DB2-4–derived tailgate complete with window (glass on the prototype, Perspex thereafter). Flooring was of aluminium and light-alloy wire-mesh stoneguards were fitted under the wings. Of minimal frontal area and with delectable proportions, the Aceca had strong overtones of the sleek berlinettas built by Touring on Ferrari 166 Le Mans and 212 Export chassis between 1950 and 1953. Given the styling origins of the Ace, the resemblance was both consistent and fortunate.

Equipped with the familiar adjustable tubular-framed bucket seats, a reasonable heating and demisting system, fully carpeted interior and a fully adjustable steering column, the Aceca was a comfortable high-speed touring car with some luggage space behind the seats and a useful range on its 13-gallon fuel tank. At 1,840lb it was 155lb heavier than the Ace, a penalty which initially caused the Aceca to be offered with a lower 3.9:1 ratio rear axle, giving the prototype VPL 441 a maximum of only 90mph at maximum engine revs.

By late spring 1955 the Aceca was well into production. The prototype was given a preliminary canter by *The Autocar* testers, who liked it very much apart from a few niggles. All AC production was now said to be on Michelin X tyres, which did give some harshness on poor surfaces at low speeds, 'but let the speed rise and the suspension is remarkable; pleasantly firm but very comfortable'. Some oversteer at the limit of adhesion was reported. (This was to be corrected by amending the rear spring to give a measure of negative camber at rest.) The testers thought the car was thoroughly practical and recorded better than 26mpg with it.

During the 1954 the light-alloy brake backplates were found to be too weak and were replaced with steel ones. A broad pressed-steel stiffening web was welded into both front and rear wishbones after signs of cracking had appeared at the welds on

The start of one of the races at Zandvoort which formed part of the Tulip Rally tests. The Ace closest to the camera was to win its class.

some of the more fiercely-driven Aces.

As 1954 drew to a close, AC Cars were in a fairly satisfactory position. They had moved almost effortlessly from making staid, worthy and quite dull saloons into a new market with two of the most convincing high performance cars of the day. With the Aceca they had a GT coupe the match of such glamorous vehicles as the Fiat 8V, Lancia Aurelia B20, Porsche 356 Super and even – perhaps – the likes of the Ferrari 166MM. From UK makers the opposition came from the Aston Martin DB2-4, Bristol 404, Frazer Nash Le Mans and Jensen 541. Experience was to show that even worldwide this was a tiny market, but then so was AC's production capacity. . .

For 1955 weekly production was set at five cars a week. Half were to go overseas – to the USA for the most part, but also to the company's energetic Parisian representative and to Switzerland, another promising market. In January 1955 it was

Some 37 years after it was first announced, the AC Six engine could still put up a respectable performance in major international endurance races. Here is the Dressel/Woodbury Ace getting away from the pits during its reliable run in the 1956 Sebring 12 Hours. The permanently installed bonnet catch keys and identification lights are notable, as is the belt running up from the car's front bumper.

An Ace on a raised display platform at an American car show showing its USA-style front bumper. The narrow cross-ply tyres mark this as an early car.

The Aceca was introduced at the 1954 Earls Court Show. The square lower corners of the windscreen frame, the whitehall tyres and the small chrome 'Aceca' scroll are notable. The USA-type bumpers on the white Ace behind were to be superseded by a straight twin-tube design on many Acecas.

An Aceca chassis-frame viewed from the rear showing the twin rear outriggers and the modified mounts for the differential housing.

The Aceca AC engine installation. The grease gun is handily placed in clips on the inner wheelarch.

announced that 60 Aces had been delivered. The compression ratio had been taken up a notch to 8.0:1, and somebody at the factory told *Motor Sport* that skimming off another 30 thou would give 8.5:1. Maximum engine revs were still officially only 4,500rpm and power was still quoted at 85bhp.

Aces began to appear in competition. John Gott took the 2-litre class in the Tulip Rally in 1955 against a flock of Triumph TR2s. There were successes in UK club racing events. AC's private owners began to face tougher opposition than they could handle on two fronts. The big makers like BMC and Triumph were now taking international rallying very seriously. Entering fleets of what Derek Hurlock saw as 'throwaway sports cars', they could take risks unacceptable to the entrants of a costly and not so easily repaired vehicle like an Ace.

The other problem was lack of power. AC Cars were pushing forward as quickly as seemed prudent with the old engine. They moved the intake to the oil pump so that it was no longer starved on the long right-handers which predominated in circuit racing. Up to chassis AE59 they used UMB or UMC units with 2000

An AC engine on long-term test prior to installation. AC went to considerable trouble to build and bed-down smooth engines throughout the power unit's production life.

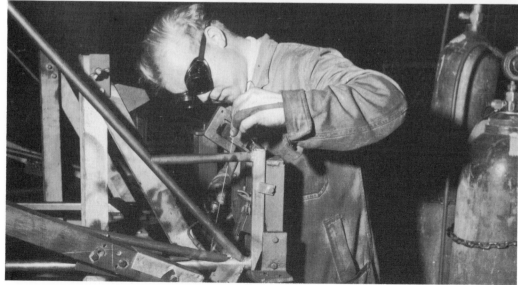

A great deal of skilled handwork went into the manufacture of ACs. Here, the rear subframe of an Aceca is being welded prior to panelling.

series numbers. Early in 1955, larger diameter crankshaft CL series motors were introduced with substantial improvements in bearing design and larger capacity oil pumps using helical gears. Power went up to 90bhp, still at 4,500rpm. There was a useful 110lb/ft of torque at 2,500rpm.

The situation was neatly illustrated in September 1955 at Oulton Park, where a Standard Production Sports Car race was held. Run over 30 laps (84 miles) the entry was limited to genuine production models costing less than £1,500. The entry included no less than 13 TR2s, six Austin-Healeys, four Morgans, a Sunbeam Alpine and six AC Aces. Eventually 11 TR2s, two Austin-Healeys, four Aces, two Morgan Plus Fours and the Alpine started. After taking the lead, the two Austin-Healeys took each other off, leaving the road clear to Peter Reece's Morgan, which duly won ahead of the Aces of Standbridge and De Mattos after the Triumphs succumbed to all sorts of maladies.

Something had to be done. As an interim step it was announced during 1956 that 5,000rpm was acceptable on the AC engine, with more possible for brief periods. AC's concern was well-founded for at these revolutions piston speed was high indeed and rocker life was limited if much more than 5,000rpm was held for long periods.

Also at this time, rubber bushes replaced the inboard bronze bushes on the suspension. External changes included a move to square rear lights; first small overriders, then full-width bumpers were offered to export purchasers. The rear line of the Ace's hood was moved aft slightly when experience showed that water could flow forward from the rear decking in the bad weather. The line was also slightly better aerodynamically. Suspension anti-roll bars, underpan cowlings and crash bars became available. There were luggage racks for the boot-lids and some cars had the handbrake down beside the seat near the door instead of the fly-off type perched high by the driver's elbow on top of the transmission tunnel.

In America, the Sebring 12-Hours endurance race had been steadily growing in importance and gave the AC-engined Ace its only opportunity to show its stamina in an endurance event. The largely standard example of Dressel and Woodbury covered 154 laps to come fourth in the 1,601-2,000cc class behind the Ferrari of Rubirosa/Pauley and two Arnolt-Bristols. It was 18th in general classification, but perhaps more importantly the AC had shown its reliability and set the pattern for a series of notable performance in the Florida classic during the next three years.

Although it had two straights of around 1,500 yards, the 5.2-miles Sebring circuit was tortuous and demanding on brakes, suspension and steering. The Ace's average speed for the 12 hours was 66.7mph. Some 29 years before, the Bruces had driven their two-seater AC Six Sports at Montlhéry track for 10 days to cover 15,000 miles at just over 68mph average. At Montlhéry there were no corners and the track was banked. Perhaps it is misleading to relate the two performances, yet they are linked by that wonderful old Light Six engine. What other manufacturer has ever had the cheek – and the consistency – to build a competitive sports car powered by a version of a motor which had broken international records three decades before?

CHAPTER 5

The Bristol-powered versions

Developing a racing heritage

The 1936 BMW 328 two-seater was a trendsetter with its soft suspension and low weight. It confirmed that the day of the harshly sprung, overweight sports car on traditional British lines was over. By 1940 they had evolved an advanced streamlined sports-racer which produced 120bhp at 5,500rpm on a 9.6:1 compression ratio from 1,971cc. With a top speed of 130mph for the open versions and 134 for the closed coupes, they were formidable performers. One of them was fifth in the 1939 Le Mans 24-Hour race, and another won the 1940 Brescia GP, substituted for the Mille Miglia. Sir Roy Feddon, technical adviser to the Ministry of Aircraft Production and the genius behind the superb Bristol aero engines of the 1920s and 1930s, studied the BMWs and their engines after the collapse of Nazi Germany and in due course the BMW designs were transferred to Bristol and Frazer Nash as war reparations. Derivatives of the BMW car were built by both companies using the six-cylinder engine. The Bristol 401 to 404-series coupes became established as expensive specialist cars with powerful engines, which because of their torque characteristics demanded energetic use of the intermediate gears.

BMW designer Fritz Fiedler had managed to include hemispherical combustion chambers with inclined valves without going to the expense of overhead camshafts. A camshaft in the block operated the inlet valves by pushrods and single rockers. The exhaust valves were opened by vertical pushrods which operated rockers actuating pushrods across the head. These pushrods moved secondary rockers which bore on the valves. Light and straightforward to maintain, the valve-gear was good for up to 6,700rpm in the form in which the unit was

used in racing and up to 6,000 in roadgoing trim. By the time AC Cars began to think of using this engine it had been more-or-less totally re-designed by the engineers at Filton. In its most basic form output was around 85bhp, but as used in Formula 2 racing from 1952, 150bhp was produced.

The cylinder head was aluminium, but the block was of chrome cast-iron, with nickel-alloy steel liners. Vanwall thinwall lead-bronze indium-plated bearings were used for both mains and big-ends. The Nitrided crankshaft was carried in four main bearings and the bore and stroke were 66 x 96mm. Like the AC unit, it was tall and narrow, especially with the three Solex carburettors feeding the vertical inlet tracts perched between the rocker covers.

Ken Rudd's determination to provide his 1954 Ace VPL 442 with enough power to trounce the TR2s and Austin-Healeys in British club racing led to this car becoming the first Ace-Bristol. He appeared with it in Bristol guise in a 13-lap Production Sports Car race at the 1956 Goodwood Easter meeting and went on to win as well as set fastest lap at 80.15mph. Rudd had an excellent 1956 racing season, finishing second to the Fitzwilliam MGA in the three-hour final race of the *Autosport* Production Sports Car Championship at Oulton Park in September and winning the series on aggregate.

AC lost no time in making the Bristol engine available. It was an expensive item and initially they planned to fit the 100C2 version, offering 105bhp. The company explained that the new powerplant was really intended for those who wanted to race. For those who merely wished to enjoy the delights of the AC on the road, their own engine would still be available. Although it

would have been possible to mate the Bristol engine to the well-tried Moss gearbox, it was decided to use Bristol's own unit, a complicated design, but very robust and sporting a constant-mesh first gear as well as synchromesh on the three other ratios. It had slightly closer ratios than the Moss box (Moss ratios in brackets): 3.6 (3.6), 4.7 (5.0), 7.2 (6.6), 12.3 (10.6). A popular option on British cars in the 1950s was the Laycock De Normanville overdrive and this was offered on both Bristol and AC-engined cars during 1956, BE577 being the first Aceca-Bristol to have it. The overdrive unit consisted of an epicyclic gear train engaged by a cone clutch operated by oil pressure from the unit's own pump. Engine braking was available and the change, controlled by a switch, occurred during full power transmission. The overdrive unit was mounted behind the gearbox.

A typical Aceca installation involved using the low 3.9:1 rear axle. The ratios then became (overdrive ratios in brackets): 3.9 (3.2), 5.43 (4.38), 7.85 (6.35), 13.5 (no o/d). Overdrive top gave 25mph per 1,000rpm, bringing the Aceca well over 100mph even if the old 4,500rpm red-line limit was observed. With overdrive AC-engined cars, the most rewarding technique for effortless high-speed cruising was to accelerate rapidly to the 80mph or so in top at which the engine was happiest and then engage the overdrive.

50

The superb straight-six Bristol engine, which transformed the Ace into one of the classic sports-racing cars of its era.

An AC Ace-Bristol display chassis, which was exhibited for the first time at the 1957 Earls Court Show.

A home-market Ace-Bristol awaiting collection by its lucky owner outside the factory showroom at Thames Ditton.

The revised rear deck with shorter boot-lid on later Aces permitted a better aerodynamic line to the hood when it was erected. The rectangular lights and small overriders were typical fittings and the lockable facia compartment was a welcome refinement.

Prices quoted for the range at the Motor Show in late 1956 were £1,100 for the Ace, £1,340 for the Ace-Bristol, £1,375 for the Aceca, £1,585 for the Aceca-Bristol, all without overdrive and with a further 50 per cent purchase tax liable on these prices. The marque was holding its market position, dearer than popular UK sports cars, but cheaper than imported machinery.

By 1957, the American market had become increasingly important to AC. Since 1954 the Sports Car Club of America had been running its Class Championship for basically standard sports cars. With the arrival of the Ace-Bristol the hard-fought E Production class, once the province of TR2, Morgan and Porsche, became AC's own. In 1957 Robert Kuhn won the series. 'It is well-known,' said *Road & Track*, in their April 1957 road test, 'that the AC-Bristol (*sic*) is the most consistent class E winner.' Their test, of an Ace-Bristol with latest D-series motor (the D-series was unique to AC), gave some clue as to why this might be so. Always inclined to develop torque at high revs, this occasionally raced engine had a 'wild' cam, with 64 degrees

52

Some owners specified a handbrake down beside the driver's seat of their Ace rather than up on the transmission tunnel.

overlap, 284 degrees duration, holding off maximum torque to an 'astounding' 5,000rpm on an engine red-lined at only 5,750rpm. This 125bhp unit gave the Ace a standing-start quarter-mile time of 16.6sec and a mean top speed of 115.2mph. '. . . This is a car which can be driven to the races in comfort, tuned for a race in 15 minutes and offers an excellent chance of bringing home a trophy'.

If the Ace was nimble and accelerative enough to be a club-racer's dream, it was also a formidable endurance racing machine, even though it competed in largely production guise at a time when most large manufacturers were energetically fielding works teams of special competition cars. At Sebring in the Florida spring, the Ace-Bristol of Fernandez/Droulers took the 1,601-2,000cc GT class and was 17th in general classification. Dressel and Woodbury returned to the fray with an Ace-Bristol and a third driver, Cullen, to finish 22nd in general classification. Ken Rudd surveyed the possibilities at Le Mans and decided the Ace-Bristol could easily be adapted to the special needs of the 24 Hour race.

As he told a meeting of the AC Owners' Club faithful

AC were represented at Le Mans in 1957 with this Ace-Bristol, which created a considerable impression for its steadiness and reliability as Ken Rudd and Peter Bolton drove it into 10th place overall.

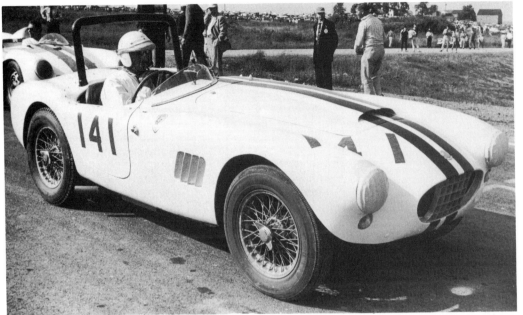

The 1957 Le Mans Ace-Bristol at Watkins Glen the following year, where it finished second in its class in the sports car Grand Prix in the hands of its new owner Dr Richard Milo. The car had been beautifully restored after being badly damaged while in transit to Sebring earlier in the year.

afterwards, he knew that if the factory was to be enticed into involvement in the 1957 race, it would have to be done on a minimal-cost basis: 'To remove the objection that otherwise would have existed – that the financial position would not permit the building of the additional car – I purchased one of the works demonstration fleet.' His Ace was 170 DPC, originally AE205 and AC-powered. It appeared at Le Mans with a Bristol 100D2 engine using 9:1 cr pistons, and the carburettors were airflowed as well as enclosed in air straighteners. All the interior trim was removed to lighten the car. A 20-gallon fuel tank went into the boot, leaving barely enough room to carry a spare wheel.

The car's wind resistance was lowered by a small air intake, underpanning in part and a low racing screen to replace the 3.5sq ft of the roadgoing one. The 3.64:1 rear axle was used with oversize Dunlop racing tyres to give an effective 3.4:1 ratio. Disc brakes had already proved their worth at Le mans and 170 DPC was the first Ace to wear them. Drum brakes were retained

at the rear. As a back-up and practice car there was old VPL 442, in full touring trim. From the beginning of practice, lap times were around 5min. The team had little trouble, recording a fastest lap of 4min 43.2sec – over 100mph – during the race and covering 2,350miles at 97mph average to finish 2nd in the 2,000cc class and 10th overall, behind a Porsche RS. It was the fastest average ever to be recorded by a Bristol-engined car during a long career at Le Mans.

The Ace-Bristol was driven to and from the race, like all other Aces which set out from Thames Ditton for the Sarthe. Back at the works the engine was stripped but nothing needed to be done. It seemed a shame to do the strip, said Rudd, and do no work, so the valves were given a touch. Fuel consumption was found to be around 16mpg at 100mph average. The Ace's effortless performance drew much favourable comment. Said *Autocourse;* 'Its timed near-130mph down the Mulsanne surprised more than a few. It must have been one of the least costly cars in the race.'

The AC-Bristol Le Mans, a specially bodied car based on a spaceframe chassis, built specifically for the 1958 24-hours race, in which it finished eighth in the hands of Peter Bolton and Dickie Stoop, despite some handling problems emanating from the swing-axle rear suspension.

The engine of the AC-Bristol Le Mans was mounted well back in the chassis, which, like that of the production Ace, was designed by John Tojeiro. Front suspension was by coil springs and tubular wishbones, coil springs also being used at the rear to control the swing axles.

The second Aceca-Bristol built was BE572, with 100D engine. It was given the 1956 registration 40 BPC and went to Tom Clarke, who took it through the incident-filled 1957 Mille Miglia as a preliminary to the 12 Hours of Reims, held on the Grand Prix circuit in July. The Aceca led the 2,000cc class, ahead of a couple of Alfa Romeos, until just 10 minutes from the finish, when a pit stop dropped them to 2nd and 16th in general classification, behind a swarm of 1300 Alfas. In the Tulip Rally, Patten in his Aceca-Bristol found himself at the start of the all-important final race round the Zandvoort circuit with a chance to win the class if he could beat the gaggle of works-supported Triumph TR3s. He led for two laps until the Triumphs moved in, 'Out for blood', in *Autosport*'s words. After a nasty moment at the hairpin, Patten dropped back and contented himself with 3rd place. 'In such a position the private owner is always in an invidious position vis-à-vis 'works drivers', said reporter John Gott.

Disc brakes were offered as a £35 option during 1957. Virtually all 1957 Ace-Bristols had the D series engine, AC

A clear view of the exhaust manifold side of a 100 D2 Bristol engine. This is engine number 1179 as prepared at the factory prior to installation.

engines continuing in the CL series – 90 bhp at 4,500rpm, and a c.r. 8:1 being quoted.

Old VPL 442 did well in the six-heat *Autosport* Production Sports Car series once again, winning and setting fastest lap at both Silverstone and Goodwood. In the three-hour final at Snetterton in October Rudd again took the Ace through to outright and easy victory, but narrowly conceded the series to 1,500cc class winner Walker in his Lotus. As had happened after Kuhn's SCCA victory, there were rumblings of discontent amongst the Ace's competitors.

During 1958 the second-series 100D2 Bristol engine became available. *Road & Track* tested a car prepared for racing with a 9:1 compression ratio and output of 130bhp. They recorded a 115mph maximum and 16.0sec for the standing quarter-mile. *The Autocar* also tested a 100D2 Ace-Bristol during 1958. These cars had the by-now unusual feature of a manual override for the automatic ignition advance and retard for use at idling speeds. Power was quoted at 125bhp and gave a 16.5sec standing quarter-mile with a mean top speed of 117mph. On acceleration, they reported, the Ace had the whip hand over

56

A triple-carburettor Bristol installation as seen from the distributor side. The immaculate appearance of this car is typical of the standards upheld by many classic AC owners.

practically anything else it was likely to meet on the road up to about 110mph. 'Thereafter it climbs more slowly to its maximum of 116-118mph (about 5,750rpm), these speeds being sustained on the test car for several miles of a high-speed Continental motorway.'

For the 1958 season small improvements to the appearance of both roadster and coupe were made. The Ace could now have a curved windscreen instead of the flat one. The Aceca had a new windscreen shape with round corners and revised guttering, the object in this case being to make the interior more watertight. With the racing cowl fitted, the Ace-Bristol now had a maximum of around 120mph. At this time production was still quoted at the five-a-week level with 10 or 12 Acecas a month being built.

Encouraged by the 1957 performance, AC Cars decided to enter a prototype design for Le Mans in 1958, backing it with a more standard Ace for the Swiss pair Patthey (the Swiss AC distributor) and Berger. Driven by Peter Bolton and Le Mans specialist Dick Stoop, the Tojeiro-designed AC Ace Le Mans was given the significant chassis number LM5000. It had a

Ace-Bristols tended to have a busy and sometimes difficult life in club racing. Bob Staples' much campaigned VPL 442 was raced, crashed, rebodied and rechassised, then raced again, having been one of the last Aces to run in a major international event. Here it is seen with its new body during a BARC event at Aintree in 1961.

An Ace-Bristol with the factory hardtop fitted was a purposeful looking sports car. The wraparound screen ensured adequate rearward visibility.

spaceframe, double wishbone/helical coil front and diagonal-pivot swing-axle rear suspension. Both entries had 100D2/S engines, tuned for reliability as much as outright power. Ex-Airspeed man Morton Cavendish and craftsman Maurice Gomm produced the aerodynamically clean, classically elegant bodywork. It pivoted fore and aft to reveal most of the mechanical components. The whole project was very rushed, the prototype having virtually no mileage on it before practice.

At 1,395lb it was a very light car and with the clean body was able to pull a top gear ratio of 3.2:1, giving it the remarkably high top speed of 154mph through the Mulsanne traps. The 1958 race opened in brilliant sunshine, but by late on the Saturday afternoon heavy rain, interspersed by periods of torrential downpour, had set in. In consequence the race was marred by accidents, although the two ACs managed to keep clear of trouble. They finished 8th and 9th overall, 2nd and 3rd in class. The prototype averaged 89mph, the Swiss Ace 88mph. As a demonstration of reliability in appalling conditions it was

creditable. But the prototype's lap speeds were disappointing even when conditions were good. Its rear chassis began to crack near the end of the race. The prototype went out again for the TT at Goodwood, but once again structural failure intervened.

At Sebring nothing had gone wrong; three Ace-Bristols ran and three finished. The least modified was that of Milo/McClure/Forlong, which was 19th overall and won the 1,601-2,000cc GT class. The fastest Ace ran as a sports car and came 15th overall at 72.6mph, driven by Stear/Norris/Harris. Harry Carter won the SCCA's 1958 E Production Class Championship with an Ace-Bristol, more rumblings from other competitors being heard off-stage, the series still being based on displacement rather than performance classes.

AC-engined Aces still appeared both in American and UK club racing. Bob Staples now had AE01 and campaigned it energetically throughout the 1958 season. Running a 9:1 compression ratio, with attention to balancing and breathing the old engine could be persuaded to perhaps 103-105bhp, but now

The Aceca's carpeted boot area offered useful luggage space for the fortunate two occupants and the wide lift-up hatch simplified loading and unloading.

was at the very limit of its powers. Rockers were the engine's weak point and in the end-of-season Snetterton 1959 Three-Hours, it was rocker trouble which brought Staples into the pits after a glorious 30 minutes in close company with Jim Clark's Lotus Elite, Dick Protheroe (XK 120), Jack Sears (Austin-Healey) and other front runners.

As Motor Show time came around again AC announced that 90 per cent of their car production was being exported. A detachable hardtop became available and was shown on the stand on a delightful bright red left-hand-drive Ace-Bristol. The racing heritage of the 100D2 engine was underlined by AC's casual statement that maximum torque was now 122lb/ft at 4,500rpm, with no suggestion that such an engine was primarily for competition use.

Further development during 1958 brought the AC CLB engine for 1959 with a claimed 102bhp at 5,000rpm on a 9:1 compression ratio. Even with attention to detail to give greater

bearing life at high speeds, these engines are strikingly harsher than earlier, less stressed units. Late in 1959 the strong but weighty old Moss gearbox which had served so well since 1936 on AC engines was supplemented by a lighter unit in which Triumph TR gears were incorporated in an all-new case of AC's own devising. First used on AEX1136, this gearbox had a 6in remote-control lever. Few owners can ever have complained about legroom on either Ace or Aceca, but the Hurlocks are a lanky breed and so with BEX1153 deeper footwell boxes appeared.

In April 1959 John Bolster tested an Aceca-Bristol for *Autosport*. This particular car, registered 598 EUR, provided John with acceleration and top speed performances which he accurately described as 'spectacular in the extreme'. By this time a purchaser could order his Bristol engine in a variety of states of tune. This Aceca had 128bhp at 5,750rpm. That was good enough to give a quite consistent 16.6sec for the standing

AC designed a logical and convenient instrument layout for the Aceca. Interior noise level in this model is sufficiently low for the radio to be audible even at high touring speeds.

On display at the 1959 Los Angeles Motor Show. The twin-tube bumpers and curved windscreen outline were identification features of late Acecas. This car had an AC engine, but the Ace alongside it was Bristol-powered.

This experimental Aceca interior was trimmed in brilliant red and white leather. The panel layout was also non-standard, with the radio being placed above the glove compartment door.

quarter-mile. Its measured top speed was 128.57mph. This car was supplied for test by Ken Rudd's AC tuning shop on the south coast, which possibly accounts for its remarkable pace. Bolster spent some time at high speed in the Aceca, 'On a day of gales and gusty winds I found the car tended to be deflected slightly at 100mph but was dead steady at 130mph. Not being an aerodynamicist I shall not attempt to explain this.'

Rudd re-appeared at Le Mans with another Ace for the 1959 24 Hours. It was a secondhand low-mileage example which belonged to one of the supporters who had attended his team in the 1957 outing. Carefully prepared to ensure that it would be as reliable as possible, the Ace was given a few crucial modifications. The factory's racing cowl went on in front, and there was some underpanning beneath. A vent to extract hot air from the engine bay was put on the body flank behind the front wheelarch and the high gearing with oversize tyres was familiar. A racing screen went on. In the hands of the experienced Ted Whiteaway and Jack Turner, the Ace just rolled steadily along. The 1959 race was run in stunning heat. Every Jaguar-engined car, all the works Ferraris and all the Porsches, disappeared. The only factory cars to finish were the Aston Martins, first and second.

In the 2-litre class the Ferrari blew up, the Triumphs put their fans through their radiators or had oil pump trouble, the

This Aceca has been substantially modified by its owner, Tony Luxton, seen here driving it close to the limit at Silverstone in 1982. The car has a Daimler V8 engine, rack-and-pinion steering and 15-inch wheels.

Open cars competing at Le Mans in 1960 looked incongruous with their mandatory tall screens. This is the Rambaux/Boutin Ace-Bristol prior to its retirement from the race; the car has survived in France and still has its special screen.

Lotus broke its suspension, the Porsches collapsed, the MG hit a dog and the Frazer Nash ended on a sandbank.

The AC hopefuls soldiered on impassively and won the class by being the only finishers. They covered 2,290 miles at 96mph average speed, finishing a fine 7th in general classification. Said DSJ of *Motor Sport* 'The AC-Bristol, used everyday as a normal sports car, was driven to and from the race and was a wonderful example of how to confound the experts and the racing world'.

To underline the AC's stamina, a trio of Ace-Bristols had already won the team prize and the 1,601-2,000cc GT class at Sebring. AC, *Autosport* approved, '. . . had covered themselves in glory, coming one, two and three in their class'.

1959 was the last season in which the Ace and Aceca were competitive in international events. Keen owners continued to drive them in every kind of contest from rallies to hill-climbs all over the world with considerable success. Staples and Sheppard-Barron were 33rd in the 1960 ADAC 1000 Kilometres race on the Nurburgring with old VPL 442. Pierre Mion won the SCCA E Production Championship in 1959 with

The Ace-Bristol prepared by the factory for its French owner to drive at Le Mans in 1962 had a smoothed nose with headlight covers and large air vents behind the wheels. It retired with clutch trouble, but survives in George Maitre's hands and is seen here in 1983 in a French ACOC event.

The Ace-Bristol with 'double bubble' hardtop driven by Wicky and Gachnang at Le Mans in 1960 finished in 22nd place. The car is seen chasing the MGA of Lund and Escott through White House.

This Zagato-bodied Ace-Bristol was built for a Swiss customer and has flared wheelarches to clear the wider wheels which have since been fitted.

his Ace-Bristol and that really was too much for the organizers, who announced that henceforward the Ace would be elevated to D Production, where the Austin-Healey Hundred and the Mercedes-Benz 300SL ruled the roost. It was to no avail, for in 1960 Elliott Pew took the D Championship with his Ace. Exasperated, the SCCA once again hiked the Ace-Bristol up a class, to C Production, where previous winners had included Jaguar XK120M, Chevrolet Corvette, and Porsche Carrera. Pierre Mion came back into the picture and once more took an Ace-Bristol through the season to win the Championship in 1961. An Ace's final appearance at Le Mans was in 1962, when the privately owned but factory prepared Ace-Bristol of Magne/Martin retired after four hours with clutch failure, that component having been attended to just before the race by a local mechanic.

By the end of 1959 AC cars had been in the sports car market for six years. The Ace and Aceca were lauded wherever enthusiastic drivers gathered for their delectable combination of elegant lines, high speed, responsive handling and carefully hand-crafted individuality. 'If the price seems high', said *Road & Track* in 1960, the fact that this is still very much an "upholstered racing car" does a lot to justify that price'. But the fact was, that despite the racing pedigree, it was not possible to actually make money from building the things in the tiny quantities determined by the orders in hand. By now the company was very good at development. There had been a steady trickly of interest in a four-seater GT car, something like the Aceca but more roomy and with covered luggage space, and slightly more supple suspension. The factory needed a wider market.

CHAPTER 6

The Greyhound and Ace 2.6

Ruddspeed and the Ford factor

Whilst the Ace and Aceca had continued in production, AC Cars had experimented with several prototypes using horizontally-opposed engines. None of these were to come to anything, although a snub-nosed prototype four-seater saloon turned up at Goodwood in 1955 and was spotted in the paddock. With its perforated disc wheels and swing-axle independent rear suspension it was a depressingly clumsy vehicle even for the mid-1950s.

The big problem for AC and designer Alan Turner, committed as they were to long straight-six engines, was that their well-tried and effective front suspension with its transverse leaf spring prevented the engine from moving forward as it would have to do if weight distribution was to be acceptable on a fully-laden four-seater. Significantly, the 1958 Ace Le Mans was given inclined helical coil front suspension and a form of swing-axle rear end. At about the same time a special wide Aceca, chassis number A86, was built with a 100D2 engine. At the front there were coil springs and rack-and-pinion steering; at the rear, twin Armstrong coil spring and damper units either side with a single low wishbone. On this car there was a vertical spare wheel because the fuel tank was now located forward, above the rear axle, and there were inboard Alfin brake drums at the rear. A Frazer Nash remote-control extension was fitted to the gearbox and as this car was to cover a considerable mileage as the personal mount of the Hurlocks, deep footwells were provided.

When, in October 1959, the new Greyhound four-seater Grand Touring saloon was announced, it could be seen to have been evolved in the light of experience with these three prototypes. In their Press advertisements, AC Cars posed themselves a question: 'may we have a four-seater sports saloon with the qualities and performance of the AC Aceca?' The answer was, 'Yes, here it is, the new AC Greyhound to answer the request of motoring connoisseurs'.

Assuming the question really was one demanding an answer, AC's response was particularly well-judged. They did not move any more than was absolutely necessary from what they knew well. Their first thoughts were to stretch the Aceca. The twin-tube chassis was extended to give a 10in increase in wheelbase; the Bristol engine was mounted well forward. Outriggers and a strong body sub-structure were of square steel tube and new suspension of wishbones and coil springs at the front, swinging arms at rear, was used. A light alloy skinned saloon body was devised.

The Greyhound prototype was not very well received at the London Show in 1959. It was also quickly evident that the chassis was not strong enough. Second thoughts led to a new square-tube frame with a stiffer network of secondary tubes to which a newly designed suspension was grafted. Rack-and-pinion steering was used. To avoid using space required for rear seat occupants, the rear suspension used a wishbone-shaped assembly with one arm to take cornering loads and a fore-and-aft arm to control brake reaction and drag. Heavy-duty Hardy Spicer double-jointed arms drove the rear hubs through a sliding shaft in the hub. The coil spring and damper units were placed well out towards the wheels and the rear brakes were outboard with Alfin drums. Although something of a compromise, it was a well-reasoned response to a quite

First thoughts on the Greyhound. This was the drawing used to illustrate the initial publicity material for the type in 1959. The production car was to differ in a number of respects, especially at the front.

Two Greyhounds, those of Humphrey and Tonkin, at an ACOC event. The bumpers on the car in the foreground are basically as used on London taxis. Many enthusiastic Ace owners moved on to the Greyhound as their families outgrew the roadster.

The Greyhound was beautifully built and luxuriously equipped with such unfamiliar items (to UK drivers) as reclining front seats. The car was very nearly a full four-seater.

On the wider wheel rims and tyres chosen for it, the Greyhound's manners are impeccable, as this picture of an example being driven by John Goose at Goodwood reveals.

A quiet rural setting for the prototype Ace 2.6, the car brought about by the marriage of the familar chassis and body with a Ford Zephyr six-cylinder engine.

complicated problem: the wheels moved in a reasonably vertical arc, there was plenty of room left for the passengers and it was easier to service than the old Ace system.

There was much thoughtful detail on the Greyhound. Twin master cylinders provided a separate braking circuit for the front brakes. There were glass-fibre reinforced panels for the boot flooring and the engine bulkhead. The interior was finished to high standards of luxurious quality and front seats were reclining ones by Reutter. An unexpected feature was the extra luggage space provided when the bottom-hinged boot-lid was left open.

AC designed their own light-alloy final-drive casing into which an ENV hypoid-bevel nose-piece was fitted. It was mounted by three rubber bushes. With a kerb weight of 21½cwt the Greyhound was provided with a rear axle ratio of 4.1:1, giving 18.5mph per 1,000rpm. Although AC announced they would supply the new car with the 105bhp version of the

1,991cc Bristol B series engine, they also offered the 128bhp D2 and a B series variant of 2.2 litres which gave only 105bhp but 129lb/ft of torque at a usefully modest 3,000rpm.

With four occupants more than half the car's weight was over the rear suspension and the Greyhound was to show itself sensitive to wheel and tyre equipment. No doubt the suspension would have been adjusted to obviate this had more than just 100 or so cars been built.

The version that went to *The Motor* to test in 1961 – production was slow to gather pace – had the D series 128bhp engine with overdrive. The testers liked the close-ratio gearbox, but thought that plenty of second and third gear use would be necessary to allow the Greyhound to show its potential in what they described as 'suburban traffic'. Interestingly, they were given two sets of tyres to compare. On Michelin X 5.50 x 15 braced-tread tyres, comfort was high and at suburban speeds gave 'delightfully instantaneous' steering response but in hard

68

The front end of Ace 2.6 chassis number RS5025 showing the extra leaf in the front spring called for by the greater weight of the Ford straight-six engine.

A rear-end view of the same chassis. It was common practice to lag the road springs on Ace and Aceca models.

driving the car's response on these radial-ply tyres, 'did not inspire confidence'.

On 6.40 x 15in Dunlop Road Speed cross-plies the riding comfort left something to be desired although there was no instability even during the 110mph high-speed runs on a damp surface. The testers concluded that further chassis improvements were desirable to obviate the dynamic problems they had identified. It was all very unfortunate. Turner had intended the car for 16in wide-rim wheels, but Charles Hurlock insisted on putting the car out for test on 15in wheels. Apart from that, the car was comfortable and good-looking. *Road & Track* had one of the 2.2-engined versions to test in 1962, close to the type's demise. They seemed to like the car, finding the body aerodynamically very clean, and suggesting one of the lowest drag figures ever. They had fewer qualms about the handling of this Michelin X-shod car although they felt there

was some rear-wheel steering. The brakes were 'superb' and the quick and positive steering gave precise control. The testers were disappointed by their performance figures. Top speed was 105mph, and the standing quarter-mile took 19sec. They thought the car might benefit from an aluminium Buick or Oldsmobile V8 engine. . .

By 1961 Bristol had decided the old engine no longer provided the power they needed for their increasingly heavy and well-equipped luxury cars. They turned to American V8 power and AC found themselves out in the cold. They did not give up easily. During 1960 they took another look at their own straight-six and from engine CLB2457 introduced a new camshaft with fiercer profile to replace that which had been used ever since 1936. The Nitrided camshaft was acknowledged with a final series of CLBN units. The last Ace with AC engine was AEX1194 with CLB2476. The CLBN was destined for the

Greyhound and Aceca, the last Aceca leaving the works in 1961 as AE822 powered by CLBN2481 to a UK purchaser. Aceca-Bristol production really ended in 1960, although a couple left later, BE816 with 100D2 1096 in March 1961 and BE819 with 100D2 1141 in October 1962. The last Ace-Bristol was one of four which left the works in 1963, well into the Cobra era. It was BE1218 with 100D2 1177 and went to Switzerland, where it is still to be seen in its first owner's care.

For all its 110bhp, the final series of AC engine clearly could never provide the power necessary for the Greyhound to make headway against the splendid specialist cars now opposing it in the market. Depending on whether you see the AC as a luxury touring car or as a race-bred GT coupe, it faced the Bristol 407 V8, the Jaguar 3.8 Mk 2 saloon, the Mercedes 220 SE coupe, Rover 3 Litre, or in a GT vein the Aston Martin DB4, Jaguar E-Type or Jensen 541S. From Italy Alfa Romeo and Lancia offered what on paper might have seemed the most direct competition, with coupes from both of around 2 litres. Given a season to work out the bugs and a lot more power, the Greyhound had promised quite well.

A stage 3 Ruddspeed conversion on the Ford Zephyr engine as fitted into an Ace 2.6.

This is the Stage 4 conversion of the Zephyr engine, featuring triple SU carburettors.

Once again, Rudd had a solution. His AC and specialist car retailing operation at Worthing now included Ruddspeed, a busy offshoot specializing in competition preparation and all the goodies dear to the enthusiast heart. He knew the Ford Zephyr-Six engine, having been involved in tuning it since the early 1950s. It was about 1950 that Ford of Dagenham introduced this modern pushrod overhead-valve six-cylinder unit with its 'oversquare' bore-stroke ratio. It went through two main variants, in 1953 powering the Monte Carlo Rally-winning Zephyr, and having a bore and stroke of 79.4mm x 76.2mm to give 2,262cc and an output of 68bhp. As produced by Ford, build quality was not particularly high and the engine needed the ultra-flexible rubber mountings on which it rode. A number of concerns offered tuning equipment for this engine, the Rubery Owen-made aluminium Raymond Mays cylinder head being one of the most notable. By the time AC Cars and Rudd began to contemplate it, swept volume was up to 2,553cc with a bore and stroke of 82.55mm x 79.5mm. As fitted in 1961 Zephyr and Zodiac saloons, power was 85bhp at 4,400rpm and maximum torque was 113lb/ft at 2,000rpm. It usually drove

through a three-speed gearbox with overdrive on the upper two ratios. With more than 56 per cent greater piston area than the Bristol and yet for all its cast-iron construction only 100lb heavier, the Zephyr engine clearly had plenty of potential.

Rudd dispensed with the three-speed Ford gearbox and reverted to the well-tried Moss four-speed one. On the first Ford 2.6 Ruddspeed Ace he made no alterations to the body lines, but put an extra leaf in the transverse front spring and used heavy-duty dampers to brace it against the engine's greater weight.

AC Cars adopted the Ruddspeed heart transplant immediately, allocating Rudd's Ace 700 BBP (AE1191) the new chassis number RS5500. Rudd schemed out a five-stage tuning programme taking the engine up to 170bhp, using three twin-choke Weber 4DCEOE carburettors, light-alloy pushrods and special lightweight high-speed pistons. Stage 1 (90bhp at 5,000rpm) used the Ruddspeed-reworked Ford cylinder head. Stage 2 (125bhp at 5,500rpm) added special high-speed pistons and light pushrods, opened and polished ports, larger inlet and exhaust valves and an improved inlet manifold with three 1½in

The Stage 5 version of the Ruddspeed conversion of the Zephyr engine, with triple Weber carburettors and claimed to offer the Ace 2.6 a power output of 170bhp.

For many enthusiasts the Ace 2.6 is the prettiest AC of them all. This example is being driven by Julia Armitage at an ACOC sprint on a wet day at Goodwood in 1982.

H4 SU carburettors. Stage 3 (130bhp at 5,000rpm) brought the six-port Raymond Mays light-alloy head, light pushrods, 9.5:1c.r. and twin SU carburettors. Stage 4 also had the light-alloy head, but added high-speed pistons and a third carburettor (150bhp at 5,500rpm). Stage 5 used the three Weber twin-choke carburettors and gave 170bhp at 5,800rpm.

In September 1961 Dennis May reported in *Car and Driver* on his experiences with 700 BBP in Stage 4, 150bhp, 154lb/ft form. In May's exuberant prose the Zephyr engine 'Snarls with fierce relish . . . it is a schizophrenic. If you want to play rough you can indulge in a screaming surfeit of revs in every gear, taking the counter needle round to the red-lined 6,000rpm mark before snatching the short back-cranked shift lever from notch to notch'. May reported that was the key to the car's split personality. In their report in August 1961 *The Motor*'s testers noted the other side of this car's character: 'The Zephyr unit gives startling pick-up from very low rpm. Not only can the car be driven at 10mph in overdrive top, but it will accelerate from this speed to 30mph in 7.3 seconds'. Admittedly, the drive-shafts complained a little . . .

The 2.6 Ford installation added about 1cwt to the Ace's weight, and made little difference to roadholding. The lower overall height of the Ford engine permitted the smoothly restyled front end first seen at the 1961 Motor Show. The 2.6 offered a top speed in roadgoing form of well over 135mph plus a standing start time of 16.6sec. In Stage 4 trim 100mph in third gear was possible.

And it was well-priced. Early in 1961 the Ace-Bristol cost £2,197 tax paid, the basic Ace 2.6 £1,747. To bring it up to 125bhp Stage 2, giving it the same output as the Bristol-powered Ace, cost £110, still a useful £347 cheaper. Even the 170bhp of the Stage 5 conversion only added £248 to the cost of the basic Ace 2.6.

Experience has shown that as a racing unit the 2.6 was seriously flawed. Long-term development would have been necessary to work out the crankshaft and main bearing weaknesses that were known to exist as early as 1962. The cylinder heads also gave problems on highly-tuned engines; certainly Rudd and AC Cars would have had to blueprint and rebuild every engine they used if they hoped to retain the immensely high reputation they had gained in the Bristol-powered days.

On the racing circuits the Ace-Bristol continued its winning way. Bob Staples now drove Rudd's old VPL 442. Tuned by Chris Lawrence, and with the suspension tweaked by Bob himself and his brother Barry, it had Koni dampers and a front suspension anti-roll bar. As the 1950s merged into the 1960s, 16in wheels became less popular with sports car manufacturers and AC followed the trend as the ranges of tyres made in 16in wheel diameter sizes dwindled. Staples took the Ace down to 15in tyres at the front, in part to part to reduce unsprung weight but also because they were cheaper, and 'to stop the tyres rubbing on the wings when we go round corners'. Even with more than 150,000 hard racing, rallying and roadgoing miles on it, the old Ace-Bristol was still sprightly enough to see off all-comers and take the BARC's Fred W. Dixon Trophy for the season-long BARC Marque Sports Car Championship.

Like many of its main competitors, the Ace had been around for a while by autumn 1961. At the Earls Court Motor Show in its sleek new long-nosed guise, the Ace 2.6 still looked the aristocrat it was. Lithe and eager but still relatively expensive, at before-tax prices of £1,550 for the Ace-Bristol and £1,220 for the Ace 2.6, it was facing tough opposition. The rally-proved Austin-Healey 3000 Mk 2 and restyled Triumph TR4 were only £824 and £750 respectively. Even amongst the Continentals few could match the Ace's beguiling combination of race-winning specification and elegance. The lissom Alfa Romeo 2000 Spider with its twin-overhead camshaft engine was one, but it cost £1,830. Yet more expensive and sturdy rather than stylish was the Frazer Nash Sebring at £2,300. The Porsche Super 90 cabriolet was £2,040. It must be admitted that by 1961 AC was losing momentum; but with the 2.6, given an energetic competition programme, they might just have been able to get the ball rolling again.

It was because business was fairly quiet on the car-building front by late 1961 at Thames Ditton that Charles and Derek Hurlock were receptive when in September they heard from a brash young American who had a proposition for them concerning the Ace. In all too short a time that proposition was to turn into the Shelby American AC Cobra. The days of the straight-six were almost over; the Ace-Bristol and its hand-built jewel of an engine were soon to be historic, admired and cherished but left behind as a new generation of sports racers from High Street Works emerged to rush to new heights of power and performance and transform the company's image almost beyond recognition.

Between 1953 and 1963 AC Cars turned out 1,059 Aces and Acecas and 82 Greyhounds. There were 228 AC-engined Aces, 150 Acecas, 466 Ace-Bristols, 169 Aceca-Bristols, 38 Ace 2.6s and eight Aceca 2.6s. Most of the Greyhounds had Bristol D2 or 110 power, although a short series of AC CLBN-powered saloons was built after the Bristol ceased to be available.

CHAPTER 7

The small-block Cobra

'Just this side of reality'

The New York Automobile Show, held in spring 1962, opened its doors against a background of rising interest in competition by the big US car companies. Apart from its traditional 'under the counter' support for the hot-rodders and stockers, Ford had a Falcon V8 and General Motors its racing Corvette. On their New York Show stand Chevrolet had the Corvair Super Spyder, a show car with 15in less than standard Corvair wheelbase, its flat-six engine with turbocharger and 150bhp driving through a four-speed manual box. There was also the XP-755 Shark, widely thought to be softening opinion for the styling of the next year's Corvette, and the Raymond Loewy-designed Studebaker Avanti. All exhibited the customary American styling excesses, their extravagance highlighted by the simplicity of the little Cobra on the Ford stand. Attired, said *Road & Track*, like its curvaceous attendant, 'in stunning pearlescent yellow', the 260 roadster was also accompanied by a conservatively-suited Carroll Shelby who was happy to confirm that orders had been taken for every Cobra being built.

The story began not much more than six months before. The account given here squares with the verifiable chronology and memories of those still available for interview who were involved at the Thames Ditton end.

By the summer of 1961 AC Cars had in their Ace chassis one of the world's best-handling, most responsive sports cars, but were uncertain about the engine to power it. Ford Motor Company of Dearborn were anxious to slough off their straight-laced image. When Lee Iacocca took over in 1960 as head of Ford Division, the main car manufacturing arm of the US company, he moved it into an aggressive high performance and competition programme to build the 'Total Performance' image the market researchers said appealed to the high-rolling young market.

Part of the programme was a short-stroke lightweight pushrod overhead valve 221cu in (3.6-litre) V8 engine derived from the 1958 'Challenger' designed by Robert Stirrat. As a unit intended for millions of cars and trucks, it was of cast-iron, a material chosen to give the production engineers few problems and avoid differential expansion, corrosion, vibration and wear snags in service, compared with the superficially more appealing aluminium.

Ford drew on the very latest foundry techniques to produce castings not much weightier than they could have been in aluminium but more consistent in quality, tougher and longer-lasting. By 1961 the small-block V8 was giving 143bhp and weighed about 470lb, not much more than the 2-litre Bristol six-cylinder. Notionally the two units were comparable in power, but the Bristol was at the end of its development life, while the Ford had hardly begun.

In this power unit, Ford were responding to a trend to high-performance small-block V8 motors which really had begun when GM executives found that the faster, sports car-equipped Chevrolet Corvair Monza was outselling the basic models. In a season or two there was also the Pontiac Le Mans and Oldsmobile Cutlass, a two-door version of the Olds compact. Ford had the Mercury Comet as a sporty edition of the Ford Falcon compact. With a small-block V8 it became the Falcon Sprint. With the shortest stroke of any engine in its class the original 221 Ford was intended for these and for the Fairlane

The Cobra 260/289, the car which was to transform the image of AC Cars, whose liaison with Carroll Shelby would put the company's products before an enthusiastic and appreciative new market. The Cobra would quickly establish itself as a classic amongst modern sports cars.

'intermediate' range. Engineer Dave Evans of Ford began quietly to build a racing variant for hard-pressed Ford entrants in stock car and hot-rodding events.

While this was going on, Carroll Hall Shelby, one-time air force pilot, failed chicken farmer, Grand Prix driver and victor at Le Mans (for Aston Martin in 1959), had been sharpening his skills as an entrepreneur. He had a dream. Back to at least 1957 he had been talking to European sports car builders and US engine builders with a view to bringing one of each together. He had looked at the Aston Martin chassis, thought about the small-block V8 Chevrolet. In 1957 he had imported some sports-racing Lister-Jaguars, replacing William Lyons' six-cylinder masterpiece with the Corvette V8 engine and doing well in 'modified class' racing in USA. But that was all too specialized. What Shelby wanted was a roadster, something to be sold in its thousands. As a denizen of Southern California, his own eyes told him the demand was there. In 1961, as Goodyear racing tyre distributor on the West Coast, he shared Santa Fe Springs premises with tuner Dean Moon. It was there, probably from journalist John Christy, that he heard of AC's engine

predicament. An Ace was borrowed. Its light bonnet hid a cavern easily capable of swallowing any Ford or GM V8.

In September 1961 he sounded out Charles Hurlock at AC Cars. The response was favourable. AC would look at an engine transplant in the Ace. Immediately Shelby spoke to Evans at Ford, who somehow got the idea that Shelby was a wealthy Texan, his package all wrapped and ready.

Shelby's timing was impeccable, for by autumn 1961 Ford were well on with a racing edition of the 260cu in (4.26-litre) XHP designed to go into the largest of the Fairlanes, the company's contender in the medium car market. Shelby got two of the new engines from the first sanction. A hack 221, air-freighted to AC Cars, was untouched. Shelby followed armed with drawings. Through the winter the work of turning an Ace chassis into the first Cobra went on. By February 1962 the prototype CSX2000 and a sister car CSX2001 were well in hand, one being track-tested before being shipped out to California without an engine. Shelby and Moon, assured by AC Cars that all was well, fell on it and within eight hours of its arrival at Los Angeles Airport CSX2001 had a single carburettor motor,

A very early Cobra 260 chassis showing the steering layout before rack-and-pinion operation was adopted. Note the rear chassis stiffening, also the outboard-mounted disc brakes all round.

The inboard rear brakes of the original Cobra 260 chassis.

XHP260-1, installed and it was rushing round an improvised circuit. Even before there was time to paint it, the roadster was in the hands of the motor journal testers. Their response was enthusiastic: 'Handling is, as might be expected by those familiar with the Ace-Bristol, superb, and rendered even more so by the Shelby modifications carried out by the AC people.' That was John Christy in *Sports Car Graphic* in May 1962.

The weak point of previous V8-engined hybrids was the 'stock' rear-end. It was to this area that AC and Shelby American directed their main attention. They put in the sturdy Salisbury differential from the E-type Jaguar with limited slip feature. Inboard brakes were installed either side of the differential casing. The nose-piece was braced at its forward end to a 3in tubular cross-member. Additional inverted-U plates and a square-tube reinforcing structure were built round the rear suspension. The wall thickness of the main chassis tubes, still 17in apart as on the Ace, was increased and there was much additional plating and stiffening throughout. Heavy-duty drive-shafts were used from the beginning. The differential was mounted on large flexible rubber bushes.

Deliveries on the first 260 roadsters were scheduled for May 1962 and AC Cars quickly constructed all the necessary jigs and fixtures to permit rapid production to begin, a task eased by the

Cobra's still strong resemblance to the Ace. For expediency the body alterations were kept to a minimum, but small wing flares were needed to clear the larger-section tyres used. Shelby's second XHP engine received a 11.0:1 compression ratio, reinforced main bearing caps, a higher-performance camshaft, solid tappets and four 45 DCOE9 Weber carburettors. Talk was of 330bhp at 7,000rpm, with torque in due proportion. With the 3.54:1 rear axle, top speed was in the region of 150mph.

The motoring journalists began to vie with each other to return the most impressive acceleration and top speed figures with the Cobra, a process that continues to the present day. Featured in their September 1962 edition, *Road & Track*'s first test was of the first inboard-braked car, painted bright Moon Yellow. By now Shelby and Ford's view of the Cobra had changed significantly, and their stance was echoed in the journals. The roadster was still a perfectly practical roadgoing machine, but its main function was as a contender for SCCA Class A – Production racing, pitted against Corvettes, Ferraris, and E-Type Jaguars.

The transverse leaf springs and suspension arms had been extended to widen the track and an additional helper leaf was included. Bishop cam steering was still used. It was on oversize 6.70 x 15 tyres at the rear, with triple-laced wire wheels and there were 12in disc brakes all round. Although early testing was with a Ford gearbox the Borg-Warner all-synchromesh unit was now used, giving ratios of 3.54, 4.99, 6.30 and 8.36:1. With the 260cu in motor in standard spec – 260bhp at 5,800rpm and 269lb/ft torque at 4,500rpm – there was a top speed of 153mph and *Road & Track* recorded a standing quarter-mile time of 13.8sec. As with other test results, it seems likely that such times were not necessarily recorded on the same occasion, or with the car in exactly the same specification.

The front end of the first car to be fitted with rack-and-pinion steering.

Inboard rear brakes were dispensed with later in 1962. When CSX2002 ran at Riverside Raceway in California in September to make the Cobra's competition debut, it had outboard discs. There had not been opportunity to homologate the car, so the Cobra was put into the Experimental Production class. Exhausts bellowed beneath the doors, there was a roll-over bar and a low racing screen. The hubs had been strengthened; but it was a sorely tried rear hub which failed, though not before the capable Billy Krause had opened up a satisfying lead over all the Corvettes in the field. It was a promising start.

During that summer the Ford Motor Company had decided to put their full resources into Shelby American and to make a serious onslaught in 1963, not only on the SCCA Championship, but also on the classic FIA endurance races in Europe and the USA. To achieve this, 100 cars had to be built before a deadline early in 1963 and accepted by the FIA. A contract for 100 cars was formally agreed between AC Cars and Shelby American in December 1962.

With the arrival of the full weight of Dearborn's technologists, the pace of development moved into top gear. Power multiplied at what must have been a bewildering rate to the Thames Ditton people; manfully, they began the long struggle to translate the flow of information from California into hardware. The Cobra's first appearance on the European motor

This Cobra 260/289 is thought to be the one despatched to Henry Ford II, which would mean that as well as the side exhaust it would have had Ace-type steering. The short boot-lid is visible, and the narrow flares around the wheelarches identify this as a Mk II Cobra.

One of Carroll Shelby's many business ventures was the Carroll Shelby School of High Performance Driving. Here he watches one of his pupils handle an early Cobra 260 through Turn 7 at Riverside, California.

show circuit was at London's Earls Court in late autumn, the roadster keeping company with Aces and Acecas. Power was quoted at the gross output figure of 260bhp at 5,800rpm, although in specification tables 320bhp at 7,200rpm was given. Either way, the Cobra was the fastest car at the show.

Ford wanted results, and wanted them fast. The company was prepared to dig deep to provide the funds to keep the ball in play, but that could have been of little use if it had not been for the calibre of the team that Shelby built up: designer Pete Brock; experienced development and race drivers Ken Miles and Dave MacDonald; Al Dowd, who kept the tide of materials flowing; Phil Remington, chief engineer at the West Coast end who worked closely with Ford's Danny Jones at Dearborn.

Later, with the arrival of the 427 chassis, AC entered the world of computer design with Klaus Arning of Ford. At AC Cars a small team of capable technicians led by Charles and Derek Hurlock and including Alan Turner and craftsmen-engineers of the calibre of Vin Davison, turned the read-outs into hardware.

Ford's interest spread. They took CSX2004 and CSX2005 and gave them to the stylists, perhaps with a plan for a more fashionable outline than the old *barchetta*. The result was XD Cobra – Gene Bordinat's Cobra roadster – and the Cougar II fastback coupe, pleasing but without any trace of true Cobra character. To the end of its life the Cobra kept that flimsy skin wrapped so snugly round its basic skeleton.

The Cobra was a brilliant concept. Its teething troubles were quickly put right. At 18cwt it had a stupendous power-to-weight ratio for a roadgoing car, but it was also very strong. With an engine well aft and the driver as well as the fuel tank well forward, a low polar moment of inertia gave it delightful handling. The Ford drive-train and good quality mechanical components made it reliable and long-lasting. Exquisitely finished, it was a beguiling queen of the showroom when it began to appear in Ford dealers across the USA.

On the other hand, the stiff leaf springs resulted in a harsh

Charles and Derek Hurlock with a bearded Stirling Moss discussing the first right-hand-drive Cobra 260. This picture was taken when Moss was still recuperating from his near-fatal 1962 accident at Goodwood, which had halted his racing career.

ride on country roads for American drivers accustomed to softer sports cars. Not everybody lived in California. The hood and sidescreens, not bad by 1955 standards in the 100mph Ace, were far from satisfactory for the 140mph Cobra in 1962 as they bowed and billowed in the slipstream. It was noisy with that uneven V8 beat. Like many thoroughbreds it was soft-mouthed; the Cobra needed skilled and sympathetic handling above regular touring speeds.

With hindsight, it is evident that by the time the Cobra appeared on AC's stand for the first time at the London Motor Show in autumn 1962, both Shelby American and Ford had changed their view of the 260. Nobody seriously believed any more that the fierce little roadster would go far in the market place. It was only necessary to take a look at the opposition:

Aston Martin DB4GT	3,670cc 302bhp at 6,000rpm	£3,400
Chevrolet Corvette Stingray	5,360cc 360bhp at 6,000rpm	–
Ferrari 250GT	2,953cc 280bhp at 7,000rpm	£4,500
Jaguar E-type	3,781cc 265bhp at 5,500rpm	£1,513
Maserati 3500GT Sebring	3,485cc 235bhp at 5,500rpm	£4,372

The Jaguar and Corvette were both new in 1962. The Italians were expensive and fast; all were equipped with luxuriously comfortable coachwork and in most cases with supple suspension of more modern design than that of the Cobra's 1953-based units. Like the Corvette, the Cobra was not offered in UK in 1962, but its US price was set at the remarkably low figure of $5,995. When the Cobra did finally become available to British purchasers in 1964 it was quoted at £2,030. These prices can have borne no relation at all to what ought to have been charged if Ford and Shelby American were to get some return on the enormous sums expended on the Cobra programme. In

81

An early Mk II Cobra with an Ace-style steering wheel and British-made instruments.

Below left, a left-hand-drive Mk II pictured in the autumn of 1962 with the Cobra dished wheel. Below, a UK-market version with an Armstrong Selectaride damper control fitted behind the gear lever.

Above, the 4,261cc (260cid) Challenger V8 engine as revealed to the UK press in October 1962. Above right, one of the 4.7-litre (289cid) engines supplied to Thames Ditton for the 1963 Le Mans cars equipped with four twin-choke Weber carburettors.

The Ed Hugus/Peter Jopp Cobra hardtop which had retired from the 1963 Le Mans race, seen later in the year at Snetterton. Note the identification lights, the trunking for the roof-mounted fuel filler and the wing spats required to cover the oversize tyres on their Dunlop peg-drive wheels. Side vents first appeared on the two Le Mans Cobras.

The Cobra 289 which Ninian Sanderson and Peter Bolton shared at Le Mans in 1963 leading a bunch of cars, including the Hugus/Jopp Cobra, into Tertre Rouge. Sanderson and Bolton finished seventh overall.

the early days Carroll Shelby had been quoted as saying that he expected to sell 1,000 Cobras a year. Instead, they sold enough to ensure homologation and place sufficient cars in enthusiastic drivers' hands to know that every important race meeting would see plenty of Cobras in contention. Just as important to many American fans was exposure in drag racing. Shelby's Dragonsnake dragsters looked after that side of the business, appearing for the first time at the 1963 Indianapolis Nationals.

The Cobra Mk II, the 289, appeared late in 1962 on car SCX2076.

The first people to test the Cobra in America were encouraged to try them out on racing circuits, where the smooth surfaces would show them to advantage. When John Bolster borrowed Shelby's own LHD specimen in May 1963 he used it only on the road and around London during his *Autosport* road test.

It was not a car, he thought, for the beginner when driven to the limit. 'One tends to be rather busy when drifting fast curves on full throttle'. At fast touring speeds the 'sheer luxury' of all that power in reserve was one of motoring's greatest sensual pleasures, he wrote. Maximum speed was 136mph and a

standing start quarter-mile took 13.8sec. It was an early sample of the new 289cu in (4.7-litre) model.

In 1963, with Ford's active support, Shelby started his attack on international racing. The crown in dispute was the FIA's Constructors' Championship, confined to Grand Touring cars meeting the limitations of Appendix J, and Ferrari was the marque to the beat. A three-car team of 260 Cobras with Dan Gurney, Skip Hudson and Dave MacDonald as drivers went to the Daytona Continental in Florida in February and demonstrated considerable pace before dropping out, two with minor electrical problems, Hudson's with the more serious flywheel burst. Shortly afterwards at Sebring with the first rack-and-pinion, 289-engined cars to race, the pattern was repeated. Driven by Gurney/Hill, Roberts/MacDonald and Miles/Spencer, the Cobras proved fast but brittle and the GT class went to Ferrari as usual.

For Le Mans in June Shelby had two Cobras, both fitted with hardtops and only mildly tuned. These cars were the first Cobras to use suspension torsion bars in racing. They were specified at Thames Ditton as AC Cobra Le Mans, CSX2130 and CSX2131. The engines were sent over from Shelby in the USA with four twin-choke Webers and were not highly tuned, giving 300 and 355bhp, which was good enough for 159 and 165mph on the Mulsanne Straight and a best lap of 4min 15.3sec. This compared with the 4.9-litre Maserati of Simon/Casner, which could do 182mph and a best lap of 3min 57.2sec. The rear window of one hardtop blew out during practice so that the sealing rubbers were supplemented by security bolts. A 3.3:1 rear axle was used and 15in Dunlop pressed-alloy centre-lock wheels fitted to give the desired overall gearing. The exhausts ended below the doors on one car, at the rear on the second, and 37.8-gallon fuel tanks were fitted. The hardtops demanded an extra short boot-lid on these cars; there was a large vent on the body side. All the usual Le Mans accoutrements were installed – roof lights, external jacking points and deeper wheelarch flares to cover the wide-section tyres.

In the lower-powered CSX2131 Peter Bolton and Ninian Sanderson rumbled round to finish 7th behind six 250P, 250GTO and 330LM V12 Ferraris and fourth in the GT category. They covered 2,592.2 miles to average 108mph. After 10 hours the left-hand drive Hugus/Jopp car retired with a broken connecting rod when in 13th place.

If this first season in international sports car racing was one to bring home to the Shelby people that the 289 showed few signs of prising loose Ferrari's grip on the championship, it was a much more satisfying picture back home. In the two major amateur racing championships organized by Sports Car Club of America, Bob Johnson and Dick Thompson were 1st in the Nationals covering the East and Mid-west ahead of Thompson's Corvette. In the Pacific Coast section the position was reversed with Dave MacDonald in 3rd place behind two Corvettes. Names later to become important in the Cobra story were already emerging. Bob Bondurant won at Denver in August, his first Cobra drive netting the GT class of the US Road Racing Championship race. Bob Holbert emerged as winner of the driver's division of the USRRC driving Porsche and Cobra, winning the GT class at Laguna Seca, 3rd at Kent, 2nd at Continental Divide. In the Elkhart Lake 500 he shared a Cobra with Ken Miles to win the large car division. And this was just the beginning. Cobras were to make A-Production events their own for seasons to come and there was little the Corvettes could

do about it. They took the USRRC, forerunner of the Can-Am series, by a wide margin.

Shelby's own efforts in US 1964 racing, said an announcement towards the end of 1963, would focus on professional events, 'Because we believe private owners should compete in SCCA races against other amateurs and that our team of professionals should race against other professionals'. Ken Miles was to become competition manager for Shelby American, continuing as team driver with Holbert and MacDonald.

Meanwhile, Ford Motor Company had commissioned Eric Broadley of Lola to design the new Ford GT which even then was planned to take over from the 289 Cobra in the classic endurance races. But Shelby was not to go empty-handed from FIA events. In September 1963 Dan Gurney took a Cobra Le Mans Replica to its first FIA victory when he won the Bridgehampton Double 500 GT race, outrunning Briggs Cunningham's E-Type Jaguars. The Cobra lapped everybody except Hansgen's E-Type. This was the first occasion on which an American engine had won a FIA race. It was not to be the last. 'With most of the bugs eliminated,' said *Road & Track*, 'the Cobra should prove interesting at Sebring and Le Mans in 1964'.

London Ford dealer John Willment entered two Cobras in the Tourist Trophy at Goodwood in the autumn of 1963, but like the Aston Martin team, the cars ran foul of the scrutineers, who thought there was insufficient clearance between the steering arms and the tyres. The Cobras were non-starters.

From late 1962 to early in 1964 there was a continual stream of modifications and improvements to the 289. Many came as a result of lessons learnt in the intense racing programme, others were adopted to make the cars more reliable and marketable in the USA. There was a gap between the first homologation contract for 100 cars which was completed in April 1963 and the new one in November 1963. During this period of 1963 AC Cars introduced the first of their own right-hand-drive 289 roadsters, and a few cars for sale to France and other Continental countries. These vehicles were identified by a 6000 number, the first being COX6001 which went to Serge Leeman in Paris during October 1963. The first one supplied to a UK purchaser was COB6005, registered APA 6B. This was set up as a fully equipped road car with heater and Armstrong Selectaride, an electrically controlled adjustable suspension damper system operated by the driver and giving four settings from 'Soft' to 'Firm'.

By this time clutch leverage had been changed to lighten pedal loads, and thicker brake discs were fitted all round. Although cars for USA had lower 3.77:1 rear axles, those built for European customers in the days before speed limits blanketed the great Continental routes retained the 3.54:1 ratio. The cast light-alloy Halibrand spline-drive wheels first seen at Daytona early in 1963 were immediately used on Cobras in the USA, tyre sizes going up from the Goodyear 6.70 on 5½in rims to 7.35 on 6in. The 289 was offered in 10 colours including metallics with a choice of three leather and carpet colours. During that summer Smiths instruments were replaced for USA-destined 289s by Stewart Warner units, and Ford started making the electrical wiring looms. An alternator became part of the specification for the second homologation contract.

The specification sheet issued by Shelby American in January

Jack Sears driving one of the 1963 Le Mans cars in the 1964 Guards International Trophy race at Brands Hatch. The rear wing now approaches the shape adopted for the FIA Cobra series and the wheels are light-alloy Halibrands with peg drive.

The same car at the Goodwood pits during the 1964 Tourist Trophy race, with Jack Sears about to climb out. The stop to change wheels and refuel took 76 seconds. The altered rear profile with the even shorter boot-lid required to clear a hardtop when fitted is very apparent in this view.

1964 for what they were now calling the Shelby Ford Cobra in the USA, quoted power as 271bhp at 5,800rpm, with torque of 269lb/ft at 4,800rpm. The car weighed 2,100lb. The close-ratio Borg-Warner T10 gearbox had ratios of 2.36, 1.61, 1.20 and 1:1, and five rear axle ratios between 4.56 and 2.72:1 as well as the standard 3.77 were available. There were dual brake master cylinders. The 72-spoke wire wheels with knock-off hubs were standard, but the Halibrand was a favourite option. At 6,500rpm top speeds between 110 and an optimistic 180mph were quoted, depending on the rear axle ratio. The price was still that remarkable $5,995.

It was quite a package, but for the competition-minded owner, it had only just begun. He could buy in Stage I, II or III, with two further options beyond that. Stage I was given some mild attention to suspension but kept the stock engine; Stage II was 'for the man who takes his racing seriously' and featured the magnesium wide-rim wheels (still the engine was stock); Stage III was, 'a team car replica. Identical in every way to the famous Shelby-American Team Cars which won the Manufacturers' Championship, the SCCA Class A Championship, the Drivers'

The FIA-specification roadster shared by Bob Bondurant and Jochen Neerpasch in the 1964 ADAC 1000 Kilometres race at the Nurburgring. Note the cutaway doors to clear the rear wing, the forward-braced roll-over hoop and the steeply sloped windscreen.

The Cobra Daytona coupe of the Willment stable, a car which was built in the UK late in 1964. It is seen here with its original nose and a domed rear screen.

Championship . . . tested personally by Ken Miles, guaranteed to equal the best lap times established by a factory team car'.

Few sporting cars can ever have been offered with such a warranty. It was available only in Stage III form with the optional IV-R engine. This $3,000 kit provided a full racing engine – fully crack-tested, balanced and blue-printed with modified pistons, large valves, special camshaft, large capacity sump and many other features. Four twin-choke Webers were added. In this trim in 1964 a good engine could provide anything from 375 to very close to 400bhp. There was also the Cobra Drag Car to NHRA regulations. With much the same engine specifications, it offered the drag enthusiast everything to bring the 289 to Top Eliminator, even including the essential 8in wide, 7.10 x 15 Goodyear slicks. The rear end had a 4.89:1 ratio and the tachometer read to 8,000rpm. Heavy-duty clutch plates were used. The four Dragonsnakes built were to be as dominant in drag racing as the roadsters were in SCCA events.

1964 opened with a new Shelby American weapon in international events. The 1963 season had shown that the 289's nimble handling and great acceleration were not enough to beat the Ferraris. At speeds above 120mph the roadster had the aerodynamics of a cellulosed brick. The Aceca had already shown that a clean coupe could do 128mph on less than 130bhp. Pete Brock called on his early experiences with GM styling studios and drew up some outlines of a coupe late in 1963. The gently sloping front decking, faired headlamps, domed roof and sharply cut-off Kamm-Everling tail were all predictable and sound aerodynamically. An innovation was the ducted tract for the radiator. Drawn in from through the low air intake, the air passed upwards through the steeply forward-sloped matrix and was expelled into the low-pressure area on top of the bonnet.

Shelby managed to sweet-talk the new Cobra coupe through FIA homologation, assuring the bureaucrats that all that had been done was to add a new skin. The reality was that Brock and his accomplices provided much needed strength to counteract the Mk II's tendency to twist and bow under the power and torque of a 400bhp race engine. At the centre the familiar transverse body hoop remained but it was now supported by triangulated stiffening members and there were thinner tubes running forward either side of the engine to the tops of the braced suspension towers. A new tubular framework around the rear suspension supported a stiff rear body hoop. More stiffness was provided by the body skin. The opportunity was taken to sit the driver lower and he was given some ventilation – although this was to be the coupe's only real shortcoming. On its 6½in front, 7½in rear Halibrand wheels, the coupe looked purposeful and proved both as fast as had been hoped and stable. The first one, CSX2287, was completed in the Shelby shop by February 1964, and the five remaining cars were shipped after chassis modification to Italy for bodies to be built there to Brock's designs. There are small differences in profile between these cars and the first one.

AC Cars also built a coupe, destined for Le Mans, introducing fewer chassis modifications but with what, on the evidence of its only outing, may have been a still more efficient body than Brock's. Late in 1964 Willment Engineering built yet another Cobra coupe. They followed Brock's designs closely and as it first appeared there was a close resemblance, despite having virtually a spaceframe chassis and different mountings for its transverse-leaf suspension.

In January the first three of five 1964 FIA roadsters arrived at Shelby American from AC Cars. Built to meet the requirements of international regulations, these had designed into them all Shelby's hard-won expertise with the 289. There was no real prospect of extracting more than 400bhp from the small-block V8 as it was campaigned in 1963, but the wide Halibrand wheels with the extra-width 8in racing Goodyears meant that larger Girling brakes could be used so that cornering and braking could be further improved. The front and rear anti-roll bars, modified steering arms and ducts to oil and differential coolers were to be expected and the external jacking points were logical. Bodies too were changed, with door openings altered to clear the bulging new rear wings and the famous little humps on the boot-lid to bring the cavity up to a size to accept the regulation 'FIA suitcase'. A series of 11 racers to USRRC specifications was also built. They resembled the FIA Cobras but were intended for domestic racing, and used pin-drive Halibrand wheels.

There was one final shot in Shelby's locker. The Brock coupe looked very promising, already recording over 170mph, compared with the open roadster's best of 155. It was light, too, at around 2,400lb, so there seemed little likelihood that the Corvettes would stem Shelby's tide in domestic racing in USA.

The Dick Thompson/Jack Sears Daytona coupe at Le Mans in 1965, with protective covers still fitted to the headlights, but with the aerodynamic fairings removed.

The previous year Jack Sears and Peter Bolton caused a considerable stir when they road-tested AC Cars' Cobra Le Mans coupe on Britain's first motorway at over 180mph prior to the 24-hour race; they are seen here with it parked in a service area. The car subsequently crashed, but has since been lovingly recreated from the remains by Barrie Bird.

But it was by no means certain that even the coupe would hold off the might of Ferrari – both in engineering and political terms – in the classic endurance races of Europe. Ferrari himself was 65, but he had in the 30-years-old Mauro Forghieri a team manager and engineer of great capability. The brilliant 250GTO might be about to run out of steam, but the rear-engined 250P prototype roadster and the 330LM Berlinetta on traditional front-engined lines were unveiled at Monza in March. By then Shelby had CSX2196, a leaf-spring roadster into which Ford's majestic 427 – 7-litre – V8 had been inserted.

The 427 went back to 1958, when it had first been built as a Ford Fairlane 332cu in unit. It had been honed to battle sharpness in the fierce arena of NASCAR stock car racing and by 1964 its power output was around 500bhp. Weighing some 200lb more than the 289 engine, the 427 was strong and reliable, with torque in due proportion. The prototype 427 Cobra showed that the basic roadster configuration still had plenty left in it, but that something drastic was necessary to improve suspension.

The international season started for Shelby with the Daytona

The Thompson/Sears Daytona coupe which finished eighth at Le Mans in 1965 was the car which had won the GT category there the previous year in the hands of Dan Gurney and Bob Bondurant, who finished a magnificent fourth overall.

Continental 1000-km race in Florida in February. The original coupe was for Holbert/MacDonald and was legal, said *Road & Track*, 'according to FIA's funny, funny rules'. It was, they thought, capable of speeds of up to 200mph. From the start the coupe sprinted away from the Ferrari 250LM of Rodriguez and the rest of the Maranello pack. Wrapped up in the coupe's skin, the rear end got very hot and the Cobra was eliminated when the differential set fire to it during a pit stop. It had set a fastest lap at 109.9mph. The best Cobra was the Johnson/Gurney roadster which finished in 4th place on seven cylinders, 16 laps behind the winning Ferrari GTO.

The Sebring 12 Hours the following month was more satisfactory. The coupe – now known as the Daytona – driven by Holbert/MacDonald was fourth overall and won the GT category ahead of the GTO Ferraris. Heartened, Shelby told the reporters the team would go out for the Manufacturer's Championship. He had in reserve the 427 roadster which ran in Miles' hands at Sebring and proved blisteringly hot while it lasted.

From then on it all went sour. Ford, not all that taken with

Shelby's idea for the Cobra 427, were fielding their own GT racers derived from Broadley's Lola with small and big block engines. Shelby had his own selection of roadsters and coupes with the 289 engines and the 427 was rumoured to appear in a new coupe at Le Mans. Between them it was all too much.

The Cobras were made to look vintage indeed in the Targa Florio as they rumbled and shook their way round the roughly surfaced, steeply cambered, merciless Sicilian course. Despite recruiting a fiery local Alfa Romeo driver in Vincenza Arena, it was Gurney's 289 which came round in 2nd place after a Porsche at the end of the first 44-mile lap. Four of the five roadsters entered retired, either in crashes or with suspension, steering and gearboxes seriously at odds. Gurney's limped into 8th place.

At Spa, the Belgian 500-km race was little better. Phil Hill's Ford GT posted fastest lap then faded and the best Cobra was Bondurant's Daytona, 9th and a lap behind Mike Parkes GTO Ferrari. Here the tail spoilers were used for the first time.

In the ADAC 1000-km event at Nurburgring five Cobras appeared. Arena crashed, Gardner fell over a ditch and Hitchcock, despite a GT lap record-breaking time of 9min

A rear view of the Willment Cobra coupe, seen here about to start an AC race at Silverstone in the company of Cobra roadsters and a pair of ME3000 coupes. The Willment car has a spaceframe chassis and modified suspension.

29.4sec, made no impression on race day. Schlesser and Attwood finally managed 23rd place and the old 644 CGT of Olthoff and Hawkins was 47th, a dozen laps after the leaders.

At Le Mans Bondurant and Gurney in their Daytona coupe, fitted with differential oil coolers (the oil circulated by Bendix pumps) rumbled round to a convincing win in the GT category and come 4th in the general classification behind Ferrari prototypes but ahead of the GTOs. AC's own 289 fitted with 355bhp engine, was timed at a useful 183mph on the Mulsanne Straight, but was eliminated when it tangled with Baghetti's Ferrari in a crash in which three spectators standing in a prohibited area were killed. A standard hardtop roadster went through to 19th place in the hands of French amateurs Magne/de Mortemart. This entry was seen as Shelby's shrewd move to avoid scrutineering problems with the rest of his cars, and was well-judged, for Ferrari were still protesting the acceptance of the Daytonas until six hours before the start on the grounds that homologation covered only 289 roadsters with hardtops, not completely new coupes.

In the Reims 12-hour race the Neerpasch/Ireland car went out with gearbox trouble and the Gurney/Bondurant coupe had head gasket failure. The Cobras showed well at the Freiburg hill-climb with Bondurant 1st GT and 4th overall and other Cobras 3rd and 5th GT. In the Tour de France the Cobras failed again, but in the RAC Tourist Trophy at Goodwood Dan Gurney's Daytona was 3rd and 1st GT after Hill (Ferrari 330P) and Piper (275 LM). The roadsters of Sears and Olthoff followed. Gurney excelled at Goodwood, getting the lumbering Daytona round the tight Sussex circuit in 11th fastest time in practice, recording 1min 27.2sec against pole man Graham Hill's 1min 24.6sec in the 330P.

None of this really mattered. Ferrari pulled his Italian strings, managed to have the Monza 500-km race cancelled and thus retained the Manufacturers' Championship. Back home the Cobras safely wrapped up the over-2-litre division of the USRRC series, Miles victor in seven races, Ed Leslie taking the other two, and Bob Johnson repeated his 1963 victory in SCCA A-Production.

Production at AC Cars continued briskly through 1964. Most cars continued to be shipped to the USA without engines. After initial problems with their own dealer network, Shelby American negotiated with Ford to operate through selected Total Performance dealers, to install engines to the required state of tune, and to service and maintain the cars. From time to time AC would make a short series of cars complete with engines and export them to European buyers.

In 1964 there were minor changes to the car: the boot-lid was shortened to stiffen the rear panel and the fuel tank was moved forward.

A few cars remained in the UK and were converted to right-hand drive. AC did not feel any strong desire to pass cars out for road test and the only 289 to be reported on by a UK journal was Ken Rudd's 1964 roadster, borrowed by *Autocar* in late 1965. The engine was quoted at 300bhp gross on a 11:1 compression ratio. The carburettor was the four-choke Holley, the rear axle ratio was 3.54:1 and intermediate ratios were 1.41, 1.78, and 2.36:1. On 5in wide, 15in wheels, the tyres were 185-15 Dunlop R6 racing for performance testing and Pirelli Cinturato for general driving. Kerb weight was 2,300lb (21.7cwt) and front/rear weight distribution was 48.7: 51.3. *Autocar* recorded their steepest-ever performance graph, with 0-100mph taking only 14.6sec and a standing-start quarter-mile 13.9sec. Acceleration indeed caused these testers to lose their customary phlegmatic calm, purple prose creeping in on one of its rare occasions, '. . . the car rocketing forward like a missile from a steam catapult accompanied by a racket akin to 100 motorcycles and three pneumatic drills all working at once'. *Autocar*'s men had captured the essence of the 289 – its dual character, combining acceleration they called 'sensational', but 'well tamed'. Suspension was vintage in character and harsh. They noticed the torque-induced twitch when the accelerator was released suddenly, and at high speeds not only did the hood begin to pull and gape from its fastenings, the top screen rail was lifting from the glass. None of that mattered: 'It is a fine-weather car for clear skies, open roads and a life away from it all'.

AC Cars had officially launched the Cobra in the UK market at the end of 1964, pricing it at £2,030 plus tax inclusive of bumperettes, heater and demister, screen wash, wire wheels and tonneau cover. But its day was nearly done. Ford had announced the Mustang early in 1964. Not unlike the 1955-57 Thunderbird in size and shape, the Mustang was available initially as a 'six', but soon, with the 289 V8 and full selection of performance options, the Mustang, not the Cobra, would be Ford's official sports car.

CHAPTER 8

The Cobra 427 and AC 428

Cubic inches and a new chassis

The 289s came close indeed to winning the 1964 GT Championship, but Ferrari and Porsche were known to be developing faster and stronger cars for 1965. Shelby worked on the specification for their new model during August. The leaf-spring 427 prototype was developed far enough to translate into production. Shelby initially ordered four cars from AC, for delivery in November. But the rethinking for the new model was so fundamental, particularly in the suspension department, that AC were given an extension until the end of the year. In the end, two new prototypes – CSX3001 and CSX3002 – were produced.

The new chassis differed from the Mk II in three major respects: it was much stronger, its chassis was stiffer and the new coil-spring suspension had longer travel.

It was a more scientific car. The Ford computers at Dearborn were kept hard at work on the design details and a flow of information swept across the Atlantic from Klaus Arning and Bob Negsted of Ford to Alan Turner and the car builders at AC. Occasionally, the distance between the two ends of the design process caused problems, like the time when the computer read-out placed the inboard upper pivot of the rear suspension just where the driver's pelvis would settle . . .

The result was the Cobra Mk III, the third generation, visually closely related to the Mk II, but as sophisticated as the earlier one was primitive. Its thick-walled, 4in diameter chassis tubes were placed some 22in apart, linked by robust cross-members and with rigid subframes at either end to support the suspension. The coil spring, unequal length wishbone suspension had anti-dive and anti-squat characteristics.

Spherical joints made it adjustable, to permit tuning of handling. Race cars were given bronze suspension bushes; road cars had rubber bushes for a measure of compliance to soften the ride.

Running gear was beefed up to match the frame. The hubs were larger and used tapered roller bearings and drive-shafts of greater torque capacity were fitted, though the Salisbury Powr-lok final-drive unit was unchanged. There were yet larger brakes and the boot was now completely filled by the 18-gallon fuel tank and huge spare wheel and tyre.

The first two prototypes were built with the soon-to-be-familiar bulging rear wings mated to the older-pattern front half-shell with 289 radiator air intake flanked by small vertical slots. The lower part of the matrix and the oil cooler protruded from its own opening beneath. The wheels were now Halibrand pin-drive and similar to those of the Ford GT40. Track was 4½in wider at front, 3½in wider at rear.

In January 1965 the 427 was officially unveiled to a duly impressed selection of journalists. Availability problems with the racing 427 engine led to some early samples of the new car receiving the smaller 390cu in (6.39-litre) unit. Some 7in wider overall than the 289, with flanks swelling out to cover the wide tyres and 7½in rims now fitted, the 427 had none of the lithe grace of the Ace, remnants of which had remained visible in the 289. Small though it was, the 427 had a ponderous, even menacing air.

At last Shelby had a chassis that, even if it was still prone to flex when provoked by that thunderous 427 engine, was three times stronger than before and, at 2,150lb, only 50lb heavier

Above left, Alan Turner (centre) confers with Shelby's men as the first of the Mk III Cobra 427s takes shape at AC Cars early in 1965. Above, the experimental 427 engine with medium-riser manifold and Holley twin accelerator pump carburettor used to test the first Mk III.

The first test session of the 427 at Silverstone was attended by Shelby American's Ray Geddes and Phil Remington and by AC's Alan Turner, Jim Reeves and Frank Fletcher.

The cast suspension upright and Halibrand wheel hubs for the Mk III Cobra.

Below left, the fully adjustable coil-spring rear suspension of the Mk III used top wishbones with trailing links. Below, the front suspension used Armstrong coil-spring/damper units, curved upper wishbones and immensely strong uprights. The hubs were adapted to the peg-drive wheels.

The 'fliptop Cobra', a development car based on a Mk II chassis, but with a 427 engine installed and used to wring out problems in the big-block engine and its drivetrain. The nose and tail sections lifted to reveal all.

overall.

The big engine weighed some 200lb more than the small-block unit it replaced. It could provide up to 150bhp more and with years of successful NASCAR competition behind it, could keep punching out the power for hours on end with reliability. It was a short-stroke pushrod overhead-valve unit with 72×101.6mm bore and stroke. In street form, power could range from 300bhp at 5,750rpm with 285lb/ft at 4,500rpm using a single four-choke Holley carburettor, to 425bhp at 6,000rpm with a compression ratio of 11.6:1. In racing form the Holley was still used but there were light-alloy heads and a fiercer camshaft. Depending on the characteristics being sought, pistons giving anything from 10.5:1 up to 14.0:1 compression ratio could be used. Solid tappets, cross-bolted main bearings, high-tensile alloy connecting rods and a modified lubrication system were used in the racing model. Another engine possibility for street cars was the 428 Special Police Interceptor, derived from the Galaxie 428cu in V8 and considerably cheaper

The bulk and brute power of the Mk III Cobra is emphasized by this picture taken at the time of the 427's launch in July 1965.

Appropriately, the Halibrand wheels of this 427 were shod with Goodyear tyres, Carroll Shelby being a longtime West Coast distributor for this tyre company.

than the 427. It still offered 390bhp at 5,200rpm, but was about 480lb heavier than the 427. The 427 came with a 3.54:1 final drive and a close-ratio gear set giving 1.29, 1.69 and 2.32:1. The 428 was geared at 3.31 in top to accommodate the lower-revving PI engine.

There were also 427 Competition and Semi-Competition versions with tuned engines going above 500bhp if required and with 3.77:1 rear ends as standard, 3.09, 3.31, 3.54, 4.09 as options. Anti-roll bars front and rear, special exhaust systems, crash bars, rear axle and engine oil coolers were all standard. Extras included a special racing bucket seat, safety harness, quick-change brake and pad kit and dry-sump kit. Competition versions stood on 7.50×15 front tyres, 9.50×15 at the rear. There was also the Dragonsnake 427 with blueprinted and tuned engine, strengthened drive-line and modified suspension.

The 427 looked good. It was already thoroughly proven and with an engine and drive-line of known capability. There would be no problem to get the thing accepted in SCCA and USRRC

An editorial assignment in California in 1965 enabled John Blunsden to become one of the first European journalists to sample the Cobra 427 in its natural environment. The 'drag strip' behind the Shelby American headquarters alongside Los Angeles International Airport provided an ideal setting for acceleration runs.

The extra weight of the 427 engine and the different suspension settings to compensate for it made the new car more of a handful than the 289. In street form there was not a lot between them in terms of top-end power, but the massive torque of the 427 called for delicate use of the accelerator.

Some of the Cobra 427s required to achieve 1965 FIA homologation on their way down the production line at Thames Ditton.

The desirable AC 289, the result of using the 4.7-litre engine in a Mk III chassis, was a logical development after the introduction of the 427.

races and championships. But there was a very big question mark over FIA homologation. Of the 100 needed to ensure FIA type acceptance, only 53 had been built by the end of February, despite AC Cars' every effort. Considering what had been done since the go-ahead the previous autumn, those 53 were a considerable achievement, but it was not enough. After the shenanigans of 1964, the FIA was determined to monitor both Ferrari and Shelby American production. As soon as it was clear that neither the Ferrari 250LM coupe nor the 427 roadster had been made in anything like the required quantities by the end of the qualifying period, they were barred from the FIA's GT Manufacturers' Championship. Shelby would have to take on the Europeans with last year's weapons and moreover now had some 50 race-specification 427 roadsters to shift. The price was set early on at the same $5,995 as the 289, but by the end of 1965 had risen to $7,000. Either way, it was stunning value for money and the price again bore as little relation to cost.

Although he had only the 1964 289 roadsters and Daytonas for the 1965 GT Championship, Shelby was also given the task

This AC 289 has been slightly customized with a padded dash and a smaller steering wheel. The offset gear lever is characteristic of the 289 installation.

Shelby American offered an enormous range of tuning and styling 'goodies' for the Mustang GT350/500 series, many of which were suitable for Cobras. This small-block 289 engine has Cobra rocker covers in place of the pressed-steel originals.

Four twin-choke Weber carburettors and Gurney-Weslake valve gear covers grace this small-block unit.

of racing Ford's prototypes by Roy Lunn in the hope that he could bring order out of the near-chaos that had reigned during the previous season. Eventually he succeeded, both in the GT Championship and with the Fords, but it wasn't easy.

The Daytona Continental in February provided a GT victory for Schlesser/Keck with a Daytona coupe. At Sebring in March Schlesser was paired with Bondurant and won the GT class. The 1,000Km race at Monza in March was organized at the last moment, which meant Ferrari had no need to go to Sebring. Ford's men were equal to the occasion, with McLaren/Miles in the Ford 3rd and Bondurant/Grant in a Daytona 1st GT ahead of Sears/Whitmore in a Cobra roadster. In May the TT transferred to Oulton Park, where Whitmore in a roadster was 1st GT and 4th overall. Bondurant managed 2nd at Spa, took the GT class at Nurburgring, and despite mixture problems due to the change in altitude, won the over 2-litre GT class at the Rossfeld hillclimb in southern Germany. He was slower than the smaller class Porsche 904, but championship points were his.

Le Mans was almost totally disastrous for the Fords and the

A Cobra 427 S/C. Shelby sold these as intermediate street/competition cars to help use up stocks of unwanted pure competition versions. The cars were given rubber suspension bushes, a 40-gallon fuel tank and front and rear jacking points. There was no cubby hole in the facia. Under the bonnet, of course, anything went, but the side exhaust and lipped wheelarches were typical.

Shelby Cobras. It all stemmed from a too-late decision by Ford that the 289 engine in their GT40 was not man enough for the job. Although the 427 went in easily, every kind of trouble from faulty aerodynamics to difficult gearboxes struck, while the Daytonas suffered a bout of cylinder head gasket problems.

The only Daytona still running at the end of the 24 hours – and with a crumpled front end – was the Thompson/Sears car which finished 8th and 2nd GT after a string of Ferraris and Porsches.

At Reims Bondurant/Schlesser won the GT category in the 12 hours with Sears/Whitmore close behind and 2nd GT. By mid-August Daytonas were 1st and 2nd FIA GT cars, and the tyre and accessory people felt free to start advertising that Shelby had won the GT Manufacturers' Championship.

In America there was jubilation, especially as 427 Cobras won four out of the six national divisions in A-Production in 1965. But the day of the AC-built Cobras ended officially in mid-season when Ford withdrew support for them. Between them, the 289 and the 427 had achieved all that had been asked. Now it was to be the turn of the GT40 in the international arena, with privately-owned Cobras in SCCA races. The Cobra continued to dominate A-production racing through to 1969, winning for the last time in 1973.

The 427 continued to be built and sold. From time to time shortage of engines meant the less aristocratic 428 had to be used but few roadgoing drivers could tell the the difference. Thames Ditton production of the 289 leaf-sprung cars ended in May and at about the same time Shelby informed them that only street 427s would be required.

The Shelby GT350 and 500 had evolved from the Mustang with Ford's blessing and from them Cobra owners were to benefit from a great range of performance options. The policy was still very much as it had been in the early days, when Shelby homologated with the FIA everything he could lay his hands on or imagine in the dark of night might someday bolt on to a Cobra.

The Cobra title belonged, through Shelby, to Ford and when they pulled back from active involvement in the Cobra programme they took it with them. AC could still use the name but chose not to for the roadsters they began to sell in the UK and on the Continent. In late spring 1966 they announced that the AC289 was now available but realized all too well that, cut off from the US market, sales prospects were small.

In the hands of the road testers the 427 began to generate superlatives. In November 1965 *Car and Driver* recalled Ken Miles' 0 – 100mph – 0mph in 13.8sec. They tried it and got 14.5sec. The car was civilized and it handled properly, thanks to the coil springs. The standing quarter-mile took all of 12.2sec. Top speed was an 'observed' 165mph. It was done with a 485bhp, twin-Holley unit with 10.4:1 compression ratio. Perhaps any modern car should have wind-up windows and a power top, they mused, but, 'its raw power, the great brakes and the advanced suspension create a vehicle with such unabashed appeal and excitement that the owner plain won't give a damn about creature comfort'.

As a road car the 427 was eminently practical. The multi-million dollar programme that honed every part of the mechanism to a high degree of perfection took out many of the problems that plagued less expensively developed cars which used high-output US engines. One problem was never really solved. The 5-gallon capacity radiator kept the engine below boiling with the help of an electric, thermostatically-controlled fan, but the occupants, cradled either side of that huge engine and gearbox, with vast exhaust pipes passing under their feet, were less well served.

Cobra production began to taper off. Shelby's last 427 was shipped in 1966, and left their showrooms some time in 1968. In England AC Cars introduced their AC 289, the coil-sprung chassis with small-block engine installed, and continued to build them in small quantities until 1968. The Cobra passed into history, but its memory is kept alive by the high proportion of surviving cars and a growing body of myth and legend.

AC Cars meanwhile had quietly found themselves a new slice of the market. In the 427 chassis they had not only seemingly limitless roadholding, but suspension that by simply altering spring rates and damper settings – both easily done – could provided a comfortable boulevard ride without losing the race-bred cornering power. Through the Cobra their marque symbol was internationally renowned. Derek Hurlock decided that a really modern-looking luxurious high speed touring car could quickly be evolved from Shelby's legacy. Under the Hurlock regime AC has had more than its fair share of beautiful cars.

The amazing 427 coupe designed by Pete Brock as a successor to the Daytona, but not actually completed until many years later, early in 1981.

A Cobra with a difference. This Ghia body was installed on a 427 chassis by John Willment in the late 1960s. Ghia built several bodies to this design for mounting on Alfa Romeo and Fiat 8V chassis.

The 428 was to be based on a 427 chassis with 7-litre V8 engine and – in this instance – automatic transmission. The adjustable suspension of the Cobra has been altered to non-adjustable with rubber bushes, and there has been some revision of the rear suspension links.

The first Frua-bodied 428 convertible. Those are triple-laced wire-spoke wheels.

104

Rear view of the first Frua-bodied convertible, showing the generous proportions of the rear screen in the erected hood.

Hurlock's good eye took him first to Bertone and then, following an introduction from one-time Ace-Bristol Le Mans driver Hubert Patthey, to Pietro Frua's studio in Turin. A 427 chassis went over to Turin early in 1965 and by mid-summer the first of the new model was back at Thames Ditton, 6in longer in the wheelbase and clad with a remarkably handsome convertible body.

Frua's credentials were good and included a lithe spyder body on a Maserati A6GCS in 1953, the Renault Floride/Caravelle, the Swiss Monteverdi, and the Maserati Mistrale. Hurlock recalls that they made no drawings and no scale models. A timber body buck was produced and whatever small adjustments were necessary were made to finished bodies. Typically Torinese, the body was all-steel, welded directly to the chassis.

On the first car, CF1 (LPH 800D), there were aluminium-skinned doors and bonnet lid, but subsequent cars all had steel skins. There was a detachable metal cover to conceal the folded hood, but that was soon discarded.

Enormous doors gave easy access to the seats of the first 428, which was equipped with a manual gearbox. The metal tonneau cover was unique to this car, the detail finish of which was excellent.

Development driving was by sales executive Keith Judd and Derek Hurlock. Alan Turner, who had striven so hard with the roadsters, was now engineering director and engineers Vin Davison and Jim Bennett carried out many of the necessary modifications to engine and suspension. CF1 at first had one of the 390cu in (6.25-litre) V8 engines, CF4 and CF5 the racing – and hard to get – 427. Remaining cars had the 428 unit mated to the Ford C6 Police automatic transmission after it was decided the clutch of the 7-litre engine was simply too heavy for the market the Frua cars were aimed at.

By the autumn of 1965 the Frua convertible was well enough sorted to be shown at the London Motor Show alongside a full-race white 427 and a roadgoing 289 Mk III. *Autocar* described it as AC 427, but the company's name for it was 428.

AC had a potential winner in the 428. It promised to be highly profitable, for development costs were minimal, the main expense of the original chassis having been down to Shelby and Ford. The price was £4,250. It was intended to build 150 cars with Frua bodies while looking for a suitable UK source. The first three 428 convertibles had the Cobra four-speed gearbox, but the fourth went over to automatic transmission. This was the first fastback, with two comfortable front seats and vestigial rear seats or voluminous luggage capacity beneath the broad sloping rear window. It was ready in time for the 1966 Geneva Show, where it appeared on the Frua stand.

The race-style adjustable suspension of the first car made detail tuning to suit the new weight distribution very simple. This one exhibited typical Mk III torque-off rear-end-induced weave. Hurlock recalls that it was not difficult to determine the correct spring rates, but there was a built-in friction element with the joints. After changing the damper rates it was found the damper shafts were being loaded. They moved to large rubber bushes instead, which also simplified servicing.

The sleek 428 was fast; a 145mph maximum was readily achieved. With huge tyres on 6in, and later 7in, wheels, roadholding was not inferior to that of the Cobra. But extended testing was needed to perfect the ride with Armstrong, the damper suppliers, and they never really found the ideal set-up.

Neither was a question of which tyres to use ever completely answered. Early cars were tried on Michelin ZX, Dunlop SP, Pirelli and Avon. AC concluded that stiffer-walled tyres were best for the car and reverted to Avons.

The 428 used a 2.88:1 rear axle and Powr-lok limited-slip differential. It was geared to do 29mph per 1,000rpm. Despite that monumental engine, fuel consumption was 16/18mpg overall during *Motor*'s demanding 1968 road test, almost as good

A later 428 convertible with a fabric hood cover and air extractor grilles behind the front wheels.

as the nominally more scientific Jaguar E-Type 2+2 and the Porsche 911L.

Perhaps because it looked so civilized the man from *The Times* newspaper got his hands on one and found himself 'Sailing along in a little over 14 seconds at 100mph with the rev-counter needle just past 3,000rpm'.

The first Frua-bodied 428 fastback was equipped with a manual gearbox. Comprehensive instrumentation was contained within a nacelle immediately ahead of the driver.

In its incompletely modified form the suspension could be caught out at high speeds on some undulating surfaces and further work went on to find a cure. At about CF23 the dampers were modified again to make the handling more predictable. Improved ventilation came in at about CF30, a U-shaped automatic transmission selector was used by CF44. From CF49 the interior was face-lifted and given a revised panel treatment to meet safety regulations. Some customers were interested in a manual-gearbox version. Clutch boosters were investigated, but led to too-lengthy clutch travel.

By March 1969 only 50 428s had been built. It was a period of severe labour unrest in Italy and Frua had its full share of stoppages. There was a substantial quality control problem with the bodies as they were delivered. The AC people were used to working with other workshops far away and developed methods of communicating during the Cobra days that were now pressed into use with Italy, though with less success. Quality of welding and fabrication was a perpetual headache. Hurlock had orders aplenty. He looked for a UK source for the body, and nearly reached agreement with Coventry Motor Panels.

The 428 was also underpriced. When AC Cars lost its Shelby American connection it was essential for the cars to pay their way, making a true contribution to the company's overheads. At £5,573 by 1968 it cost more than the Aston Martin DB6 (£4,229), Jensen Interceptor (£4,460) and Jaguar 4.2 E-Type

Two 428 chassis were sent to Ghia in Italy, and one result was this AC 428 Spider, which appeared at the Turin Show in November 1965.

A choice of open or closed bodywork, and magnesium alloy or chromed wire-spoke wheels. AC 428s were built and supplied very much to customers' individual tastes.

The luxurious high-backed seating in the 428 fastback saloon, this example of which is equipped with automatic transmission.

Coupe, (£2,225), but less than exotics such as Ferrari, Maserati, Lamborghini and Monteverdi. Hurlock believed that he could continue to sell 428s in small numbers at the existing prices, but that policy would steadily drain capital. He was uncertain that a higher-priced version would succeed.

But the Arab oil embargo and subsequent threefold price increase of oil, impending USA and EEC regulations over exhaust emissions and Ford's unwillingness to continue to deal directly from Dearborn, were all to conspire against the 428. Hurlock reluctantly ended its production in 1973.

CHAPTER 9

The Cobra replicas and AC Mk IV

There is life after legislation

As the 1960s receded into history and the legislators imposed ever-more restrictive regulations on car manufacturers, the Cobra era was recalled as a Golden Age of high performance. Nostalgia and self-interest combined to hoist the value of all variants of the Cobra to spectacular levels. Global inflation was the main cause. As money lost its value the day of the 'alternative investment' dawned, paintings, antiques, veteran motor vehicles and other bric-a-brac took the place of stocks and other securities.

In a flood of nostalgic articles the Cobra became the archetypal 'muscle car'. Its functional brawn and no-nonsense, individual character were admired to the detriment of its de-toxed, impact-absorbing successors.

AC Cars moved with the times. In 1973 they introduced the ME3000 coupe with mid-located Ford 'Essex' V6 3-litre engine, but the car demonstrated the dilemma of modern sports car designers. It was compact, habitable and had good cornering power, but, built to meet international regulations, it was no lightweight and with its half-strangled engine, sadly short of power.

Unlike many other top-value classics, the Cobra was easily copied. The shrewd philosophy behind it was that its engine and running gear were readily and cheaply obtained. Unsurprisingly a whole collection of Cobra replicas has appeared at intervals during the past 15 years, their promoters eager to cash in on the Cobra boom. Many were offered as self-build kits, their moulded glass-fibre shells sometimes of very authentic appearance clothing less convincing underthings.

Kits came with early or late-shape bodies to choice, some even incorporated genuine items supplied by Cobra Parts of Surrey. The BRA features a square-tube chassis and MGB mechanicals. From Conneticut, the ERA 427SC Shelby Cobra Replica sports a Ford 428 Police Interceptor powerplant. Then there is the Contemporary Cobra, the Python, and the Stallion from California. Whatever their merits, all were strictly unofficial.

Brian Angliss at Cobra Parts began to supply spares and engineering services to Cobra owners in the early 1970s, mainly USA-sourced materials since AC Cars had never carried a very complete inventory for the Cobra even in the days when they were building it.

By early 1975 Angliss had progressed from merely repairing the cars to the fabrication of new ones, using AC Cars chassis as patterns and keeping the identity of existing Cobras, often little more than a tangle of wreckage and a legible registration book.

One such was classic car dealer Rod Leach's COB 1, rebuilt as closely as possible to the original pattern from one of the very last 1968 chassis built up after production had ended and equipped with a pseudo-vintage body for a film.

Angliss had begun to develop the Cobra design. The chassis was stiffened using 10-gauge solid-drawn tube instead of the thinner material of the Thames Ditton products. Ventilated disc brakes were used. Angliss worked to very high standards and built a useful connection with AC Cars. With time, original jigs and tools were transferred to Cobra Parts and others were traced back to the sub-contractors used between 1962 and 1966. The correct pattern, 2¼ turns lock-to-lock steering gear was once again obtained from Cam Gears. Angliss' reputation grew, particularly in the USA.

The announcement of the mid-engined 3000 coupe marked a complete departure from the traditional for AC Cars, and development of this design was destined to last several years. Changes already evident since the prototype was unveiled include different wheels and door handles.

Cobra Parts became C.P. Autokraft and new premises on the Brooklands Industrial Estate were rented close to the remnants of the old track where so much AC history had been written half a century before. The car restoration business was separated from the manufacturing side under Emilio Garcia. In 1978 the Chicago-based Richard Buxbaum agreed with Angliss that a series of Cobras be built as new cars, keeping as close as possible to the original specifications, modifying only where it seemed desirable to eliminate a weak feature or to meet the new regulations.

In February 1982 there was a legal agreement in which AC Cars permitted Autokraft, 'on an exclusive basis during the period of this agreement to utilise and exploit . . . the use of the trademark AC'. The agreement is for 25 years and is confined to Cobra-shaped cars. Late in 1983 Autokraft were able to announce that the first production cars were ready and the company took a stand at the Motorfair exhibition at Earls Court in London where the AC symbol was much in evidence.

Modifications continued. Chassis were beefed up further by using 12 gauge cold-drawn tube for the 4in main members. The hand-rolled bodywork was of 16-gauge light alloy. The stainless steel bumpers were mounted on telescopic struts. Front discs were still ventilated, ball-joints were used for the inboard front wishbone joints and on the rear wishbones. With 3.3 turns to the 24ft turning circle the steering rack reverted to the 428 ratio.

The engine was Ford's able successor to the 289 and the 427, the 302 HO V8 of 302cu in (4,948cc). It was available in Ford Motorsport options to buyer's choice and could, they claimed, give anything from the basic 220bhp to 600bhp. To dispose of the heat such outputs generate a large capacity radiator was canted forward in the nose. A Borg-Warner T5 all-synchromesh gearbox was employed.

Although the bodywork looks identical to the 7-litre Cobra, the cockpit area is greater; under the skin there have been many changes to meet current regulations. Burst-proof locks and side intrusion-resisting beams are installed, the fuel tank has been relocated forward to a safer position, there is a much improved floor and foot-box arrangement which is intended not only to be

This ex-Ian Richardson Mk III 289 was the last right-hand-drive Cobra to be produced by AC Cars in rolling chassis form.

One of the last Cobra 427s, a car which provides the link between the Mk IIIs produced at Thames Ditton and the AC Mk IVs assembled by the Autokraft operation.

Not so much a replica as a re-created Cobra, the AC Mk IV is close to the Mk III in outward appearance. This one, with Boss Mustang engine and about 300bhp, was destined for America. Price, from Brian Angliss' works, about £25,000.

Recognizable but different – Mk IV cockpit is four inches wider and six inches longer than the Cobra's. Much of the switchgear, including the central warning light cluster and the heater controls, are ex-Triumph Dolomite. Head restraints are detachable.

waterproof but to give better heat insulation.

As 1984 opened it was announced that Ford had agreed to distribute the AC Mk IV throughout the USA. It had passed American certification and in a fascinating reversion to the function of the original Shelby American policy, would be used to draw customers into the 5,000 Ford showrooms across the nation. For the present the Mk IV is denied the Cobra title, but there is a kind of justice in that, for perhaps the AC symbol will be more closely associated with the car in the USA, where in the 1960s it was policy to suppress it in favour of Shelby's name.

CHAPTER 10

AC purchase and ownership

The choice, the examination and the road test

This *Collector's Guide* has dealt with vehicles of wildly varying character and performance, from the refined and conservative 1947 Two Litre Saloon to the 1964 289 Daytona Coupe, a stark, sports-racing projectile. But there are threads linking each part of the story. The Two Litre's engine and gearbox went into the 1953 Ace, the Ace became the Cobra, the Cobra devolved into the luxurious 428. Thames Ditton's products are the true breed of high-performance cars which reward the long-term owner in a host of subtle ways. By 1980s' standards the cars built between 1947 and 1973 may have ridiculously short servicing intervals – the Ace particularly so, with its 800-mile period – but there is the advantage that owners become really familiar with their ACs. In this case familiarity breeds not contempt but understanding, even admiration.

Although the survival rate of the Two Litre is poor, that of other ACs is very high. So greatly desired is the Cobra that it can only be a matter of time before more 'survive' than were originally built. With arrival of the Autokraft-built Mk IV roadster there is the even stranger situation of a brand-new car going into production as an improved version of the original after a break of some 16 years, using many of the original AC tools and drawings with their approval.

Ownership of a car such as the AC is not to be undertaken lightly. The Two Litre is now 30 years old and although not highly stressed, in old age may provide an owner with perplexing problems. The Ace/Cobra family was developed from a pure sports-racer which was seen in its day as sophisticated and complex. An intending purchaser should first glean as much background information as possible. Although much has been written about the Cobra, the earlier vehicles are less well served. This has been partly rectified in recent years (see the list on page 120). The most objective reports were in *Autocar* and *Motor* in the UK and in *Road & Track* and *Car and Driver* in USA. John Bolster's accounts in *Autosport* are good at projecting the feel of the cars – he was an Aceca owner at one time.

The newcomer should carefully examine and drive, if possible for some distance, any AC he is thinking of buying. Only about a thousand each of Two-Litre, Ace/Aceca and Cobra were made. The sports cars were exported mainly to USA, but also to Continental Europe and other parts of the globe. At any moment only a very few will be available and that means a would-be buyer may have to be patient. Try not to judge them by the standards of the 1980s. Suspension with stiff springs and short travel gives a pitching ride; steering without rack and pinion may lack precision.

Restoration costs seem frighteningly high. All Cobras are enormously costly to buy. But the fact is that when Shelby American sold them they were cheap. They were easy to make and are easy to service. The Ford V8 engines and beefed-up production-sourced running gear are very durable indeed. Cobra items are not difficult to locate and generally none too expensive. Aces and Acecas with much the same structure as the Mk II Cobra yet a third of the market value use engines which can be more costly to rebuild. The Bristol unit, built by an aviation company to the highest quality standards, is one of the finest designs of its era but demands high revolutions, and is expensive to maintain at an appropriate level if driven

A nostalgic line-up of immaculately presented Two Litre saloons at a concours event. Fortunate indeed would be the person who found such a car for sale in similar condition.

competitively – a role in which it excels – or enthusiastically for very long distances on the highway.

The Two Litre, of which good examples can be obtained for perhaps one-twentieth of the price of a good Cobra, would cost far in excess of its value to restore if the timber body frame is rotted. Even an engine rebuild by a reputable specialist can take more than the whole car is worth. All of which suggests that the intending purchaser should think deeply before investing. An AC is not for everybody, even if the Ace and Aceca are amongst the most delicately good-looking sports cars ever built and match their looks with performance and craftsman-built quality. Given regular and committed attention they will repay their owners with exhilarating motoring matched by few other marques.

Two Litre series

When it was in production the Two Litre was seen as a conservative, well-equipped medium-priced family car. It was low-built and stable. We might consider it heavy for a 16HP but in 1947 its acceleration and maximum speed were respectable. Modern drivers might find themselves low-placed behind the long bonnet, but visibly is quite acceptable and driving is troublefree in modern traffic if it is remembered that cross-ply tyres only are available for those with 17in wheels. There is a blind spot in the rear quarters and wing mirrors are essential for safe lane-changes on motorways. The car shows its age in the heating and ventilation. It is still possible to obtain electric windscreen demisters as an accessory and they are helpful in wintry conditions. With only weak syncromesh on the upper ratios, the gearbox calls for some measure of double-declutching changing down. The beam axles front and rear give enjoyable handling but feel potholes and ripples on corners. The latter may result in small and easily controlled sideways twitch at the rear, but with its low roll centres the Two Litre has higher cornering power than its looks imply.

All mechanical parts except AC's engine were sourced from reputable outside suppliers. Provided that the servicing recommendations are followed, the running gear and steering

The Aceca, like the Ace, is a car to be enjoyed in competitions as much as on the road, and examples are regularly to be seen in action in British club events.

will go for very long periods between overhauls. The separate chassis frame is not greatly prone to rust in the main members but the area aft of the rear axle is at risk and the mid-chassis outriggers may be vulnerable. The chassis is quite cheap to rebuild at one of the specialist restorers. Spring pivots and trunnions eventually wear out despite the most careful attention. Replacement king-pins are available from several sources, since the axle was used by other marques; spring shackle pins and trunnion bearings might have to be specially made. Electrical items last well in UK conditions, sometimes less well in hot or cold climates. Wiring looms should be replaced on all but the lowest mileage cars.

Although the AC engine was a sound design and many examples are known to do well over 100,000 miles between major overhauls with modern oils and fuel, the aluminium cylinder block is liable to terminal electrolytic corrosion. A replacement programme is in hand by an ACOC member. In the meantime owners should use a corrosion-inhibiting additive to stabilize the condition.

In this writer's view, total body restoration of the Two Litre AC is not an economic proposition. Like all composite bodies using timber frame and metal panelling, they call for quantities of skilled and costly man-hours which the final value of even the most successful restoration would not justify.

The coachwork is prone to wood-rot and metal corrosion throughout the lower part of the structure. Tell-tale signs include any tendency of the door pillars – front or rear – to give or flex or for the doors to sag when opened. Cracked panelling around window or boot apertures is usually due to faulty frame joints or rotted timber; damp as well as dry rot is a risk. As a fungus condition the latter is particularly unwelcome. In UK housebuilding practice the rule is to cut out all material from an area three feet all round the dry rot, which would take out much of an automobile's structure . . .

Despite all that, the AC Two Litre is worthy of the attention of the fastidious enthusiast. Like all Hurlock cars, it is an enjoyable driving machine and is good value for money, provided the would-be purchaser takes care.

115

C. Browning at speed in his Frua-bodied AC 428 fastback, another example of an enthusiastic owner letting his car loose on a race track.

Ace and Aceca, Greyhound

The Ace and Aceca family were seen as thinly disguised sports-racers. AC Cars did the conversion to roadgoing trim so well they are thoroughly rewarding to use today in all but the worst of winter motorway conditions, when the driver may be uneasily aware of the vulnerability of the lovingly formed aluminium eggshell around him. The Ace's leathercloth hood and rigid plastic sidescreens cope with the worst downpours though they are not entirely waterproof. The Aceca is more protective, can be waterproof, and is not unduly noisy even at high cruising speeds. Visibility is good in both types, particularly compared with aggressively styled modern sporting designs. The moulded plastic rear window of the coupe can become opaque with age but polishing can correct it without making a permanent cure. Replacements can be obtained. Hardtops are available for the Ace. Where fitted, the fresh-air heating and demisting arrangements are adequate.

Servicing intervals as set out in the instruction book must be followed. The suspension must be maintained on the top line if steering, stability at high speed and cornering are not to be impaired. Suspension bush wear soon shows in an uneasy rear-end steering effect. Worn suspension bushes can be replaced by the amateur although use of a reamer is called for. Gearbox and drive-line are long-standing, but wear on steering linkages and on splines of wheels and hubs may be rapid on cars that have been used in competition.

The chassis is of thick walled cold-drawn tube. Rust is not a major problem, although it is frequently found in limited areas of the secondary network of tubes supporting the body. Areas particularly at risk are around the wheelarches, near the battery, above and behind the differential. The sheet steel outriggers of the Aceca should be examined. The aluminium skin may corrode where it is in contact with steel in the presence of water. Above the headlamps and low on the rear wheelarch are favourite rust spots. The floors are of light alloy and corrode under the seats around the seat bolts and across the boot floor. Replacement by the amateur restorer is straightforward. The body cannot be removed from the chassis without cutting through the supporting frame at several points.

It is not always easy to identify crash damage. The stiff main

116

chassis does not seem to suffer greatly in most front or rear-end impacts. Instead, the body folds and the suspension units absorb the impact. If there is trouble it will be shown up if the car is placed on a smooth, level surface and wheel alignments studied from several angles. Interior finish, trim and equipment are of good quality with much use of leather, particularly in the Aceca. Damp thrown by rear wheels can seep into the body at the level of the driver's shoulder and damage trim in that area.

In the Ace and Aceca the AC, Bristol and Ford 2.6 engines are all perfectly satisfactory. In good tune the AC unit is very flexible, its narrow inlet tracts speeding gas acceleration to the benefit of mid-range torque. Although the least powerful option it is smooth and holds its tune. Provided the crankshaft is not cracked and the block is in good condition, overhaul holds few terrors. The Bristol delivers its torque further up the rev-range and energetic use of the gearbox transforms the Ace with this engine. It is costly to rebuild but very rewarding. In this context the Ford 2.6 in standard Dagenham build is only adequate – it is inherently a rough, coarse engine – but careful blueprinting-type reconditioning is worth contemplating. Tuning and rebuild costs can be modest at lower stages of tune, but more ambitious work requires much expenditure of time and know-how, which is never cheap.

As a full four-seater the Greyhound is less nimble than its sisters. Its steel chassis, though different from the others, follows similar patterns of corrosion and wear. There are rust weak-spots at the front jacking points. The Greyhound is also skinned with aluminium. Contemporary testers were sometimes critical of its handling. Owners now discount this; factors such as wheel and tyre choice have a major bearing on its road manners. Six inch Cobra rims with 185-section radials are a favoured choice with more enthusiastic owners.

Shelby American AC Cobra 289 and 427, AC 428 Frua

The only Cobras likely to be available are the roadsters. Apart from the sports-racing coupes of 1964 there is one Willment-built Cobra with Ghia coupe body. Hardtops are available for roadsters. Despite the excitement they generate and their undoubted merits as the final flowering of unrestricted sports-car design, the Cobras are less practical as day-to-day road cars than the Ace. But for those who crave total performance the Cobra is the answer. It is highly responsive in skilled hands and responds totally to the mood of the driver. The most aggressively tuned Cobra is capable of slipping through the busy streets of a city with little fuss. The leaf-spring Mk I and II are harsher in ride than the coil-spring Mk III but there are many with experience of both types who prefer the earlier chassis for its general response.

Designed to withstand the worst that NASCAR tuned engines could do, the gearboxes, transmissions and drive-lines of Cobras have a big margin of strength in normal use. Large or small, the V8 engines are arguable the most brilliant ever to appear from the USA. In broad terms, a good Cobra should be everlasting.

Though meant for an entirely different market, the AC 428 was closely related to the Cobra. The handsome Frua convertible or fastback coupe body is of all-steel construction, superbly equipped, beautifully finished. AC knew a thing or two about very fast cars by the time they introduced it, with all the experience of Cobra development on road and track to draw on. Significantly, the 428 has remained a favourite of AC chairman Derek Hurlock.

Rust in its elaborate body is the biggest problem. 'It's built of Italian washing-machine steel,' says one owner. 'It rusts continually everywhere you can't see, 6in beneath the skin.' That may be an exaggeration, but rust is seldom far away on a 428. The would-be 428 owner may care to balance that problem against the fact that he will command a tamed version of one of the greatest front-engined sports-racing cars ever built.

Some, but not all, 428s overheat both oil and water, particularly if driven at more than 120mph for long distances. Most were fitted with an excellent automatic gearbox, the clutch pedal pressures of a manual version being thought too great in a car of this type. With the same mechanism as the Cobra, the 428 has always looked to this writer to be an AC 'Best Buy'. That is as far as cars built after 1940 are concerned . . .

CHAPTER 11

Maintenance and fellowship

Spares, clubs and specialists

Since buying a 1936 AC convertible in 1967 – I still have it – my particular weakness has been for ACs of that particular period although there is a 1956 Aceca in the garage as well. Keeping them on the road long-term breeds a kind of sturdy independence. You become self-reliant or go under. As a member of the council of the AC Owners' Club I meet a good cross-section of newcomers to the marque. It's very touching sometimes to see the hurt bewilderment in the eyes of someone who has left the all-embracing security of say the MG Owners' Club when he discovers that replacement Ace body sections don't exist, and neither do short engines for a CL-series Aceca.

Those are facts of life. No matter how well-organized the owners' clubs, how sympathetic the manufacturer, any marque of which only 4,000 examples have been built in more than 50 years is going to give problems to those who would restore or properly maintain. The AC Cars people at Thames Ditton have always taken a lively interest in their older products. They have long stocked a useful selection of consumable parts, particularly for the Two Litre, Ace/Aceca and Greyhound. There cannot be many companies which can supply cylinder head gaskets for 50-year-old engines by return of post. The position is different in the Cobra's case, for the engines of the great majority were installed in USA and AC Cars has never held a substantial inventory for them. We will return to Cobra back-up later in this chapter.

The quickest, least heartbreaking way to obtain specialist marque expertise is to join the appropriate owners' club. There are two good ones in our little world. Oldest is the AC Owners' Club, founded in 1949 in UK and catering for more than 500 members with AC cars from Edwardian days to 1984. It provides a full programme of social and competitive events through the year. A wealth of technical information is available from ACOC, either through its publications or informally by conversation with more knowledgeable members.

The club is steadily increasing its emphasis on technical support and parts to keep the cars on the road. Registers cater for each model and there are ACOC Centres in USA (West and East), Australia, France, Germany, Holland and Switzerland.

Younger than the ACOC but much bigger, the Shelby American Automobile Club caters for all the enticing machines dreamed up by Carroll Shelby's organization between 1962 and 1970 and is one of the major one-make clubs in the USA. It runs every imaginable event, but is particularly strong on technical information and sources for the enormous variety of parts and tuning equipment for Cobras. There are active regions throughout America and most Cobra owners have, it appears, become SAAC members.

Whilst preparing this chapter I took the opportunity to discuss parts policy both with the AC Cars experts and with ACOC's own spares co-ordinator Chris Browning. Chris energetically maintains a close connection with the factory and with important other sources in UK such as Brian Angliss of Autokraft at Weybridge. As he points out, the major components used on AC cars were also widely used on other British marques: Moss gearboxes, ENV differentials, Bishop steering gear, Smiths instruments, Lucas electrical parts. Owners prepared to trawl the usual classic car parts sources – they advertise widely in the old-car journals – will often find

what they need at low cost. Autojumbles (Swap meets in USA) and classic car shows are also useful.

The problems come when components unique to the AC must be replaced. Apart from the AC cylinder head gasket sets, the factory has kept stocks of suspension pivot bushes and pins for the Ace/Aceca, Hardy Spicer U-jointed drive-shafts, 7:1 compression ratio pistons (9:1 are available elsewhere), sparking plugs, distributor points and other items. Stocks are beginning to dwindle at Hampton Court, but it is now ACOC policy to take over the factory's role. Parts are bought in from AC Cars or other stockists. Batch production is underwritten when a demand appears. Available from Club sources are Ace to Greyhound chassis sections or fabrications to original specification, AC camshaft and rocker shafts, steering box stays, main bearings for CL-series AC engines.

The Bristol company is still an important resource for maintenance and overhaul of their engines and supplies of parts. Their work is of very high quality and costly. There is a network of smaller specialist concerns which by dint of lower overheads or use of reconditioned parts, offer less expensive facilities.

The last AC-Bristol, which has been owned by Jacques de Wurstemberger since new. The car is pictured at the AC International Rally in Switzerland in 1982.

The tubular chassis of an Ace is in no sense an excessively complicated structure so that a complete strip-and-rebuild of a roadster is less awesome a task than with many other sports cars.

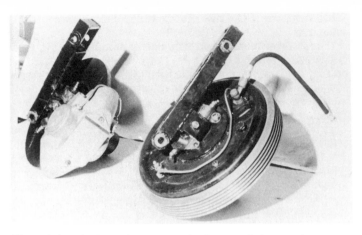

Disc-and-drum brake equipment gave the Ace superlative stopping power. The steel backplates of the drum brakes were soon replaced by light-alloy plates.

Chris Browning can often advise in the light of owners's experiences.

Other items supplied by ACOC include an appropriate pattern aero screen and small inset cowls used in the radiator air intakes of racing Aces. Ace/Aceca tubular bumpers are another project, and rubber windscreen sealing strips for early Acecas have been produced on specially-made dies. The Two Litre requires a variety of small rubber sealing strips and this continuing need is gradually being satisfied.

On sporting machines brakes and wheels are hard-working. The spares co-ordinator can advise on specialists who will sleeve and bore hard-to-replace brake cylinders or rebuild and recut splined hubs. At one point AC Cars were advising Ace owners to go down to 15in wheels from the original 16 in, but the tyre situation has eased in recent years and a choice of 16in braced-tread covers is now available.

The biggest headache for AC engine owners is the cylinder block. Early examples are prone to corrosion, although in the Ace period better alloys were used. The Club tried to set up a block-casting project some time ago without success and now a Swiss member has enterprisingly had patterns taken from a prewar UMB series block and has made castings using modern corrosion-resistant alloys to exactly prewar design. It is probable that the patterns will later be given the slight alterations to change them to the post-1946 design.

Cobra and 428 owners benefit from the continuing high level of interest in them and there are several sources for parts. They can be obtained in USA, or more conveniently for European owners, through factors in UK or in Germany. The high level of activity at Autokraft in connection with the Mk IV can only be helpful, for although the car's essential character has not changed, there has been much improvement in detail. Items such as the sealed-for-life suspension ball-joints are far superior to the equipment originally used. Modifications of this kind are similar to alterations carried out by some of the dedicated teams that campaign Cobras in Historic racing events.

Background reading

In 1952 AC published *The History of AC Cars Ltd*, by then sales manager Jock Henderson, which was a pithy account of the tale until then and is a small collector's item today. In 1976 there was the Foulis Mini-Marque History series *AC*, by Martyn Watkins, which took the story to the 428.

My own *AC and Cobra* (Dalton Watson, 1982) is still in print and is an exhaustive picture history. All models including the ME3000, AC's current offering, were covered in depth. Brooklands Books have promised one of their collections of reprints of road tests and technical articles on the Ace and Greyhound family for late 1984.

Cobra owners have Brooklands' *AC Cobra 1962-1969* to browse through. In America, Motorbooks International published Wallace A. Wyss's *Shelby's Wildlife*, and Carroll Shelby's *The Cobra Story*, co-authored by John Bentley, a characteristically breezy version of the Cobra story. A valuable handbook is Richard J Kopec's *Shelby American Guide*, a developmental and technical history of all the cars from Shelby from 1962-1970. It was published by SAAC. *Carroll Shelby's Racing Cobras*, by Friedman and Christy gives an American slant to the racing story and is lavishly illustrated. It was co-published by the Newport Press and Osprey in 1982. More recently, Trevor Legate's *Cobra* (Haynes Publishing) is handsomely illustrated and deals with the adventures of an interesting cross-section of cars.

Addresses

AC Owners' Club
Membership Secretary
Tudor House
Manor Rd, Gt Bowden
Market Harborough
Leicestershire, UK

Shelby American Automobile Club
22 Olmstead Rd
West Redding
Conneticut
06896, USA

Ace and Aceca

AC Cars, Sumner Road, Thames Ditton, Surrey KT7 0RD. Most consumable items: suspension pivots, king-pins, bearings, drive-shafts, cylinder head gaskets, 7:1 cr piston, etc. Availability varies.

AC Owners' Club, Spares Co-ordinator Chris Browning, Lower Roughwood Mill, Hassall, Cheshire. Supervises and underwrites the production of small batches of mechanical and body items from many sources. Stock position changes continually. 1984 items included steering box stays, AC rocker shafts, AC engine main bearings (CL series), Ace/Aceca radiator grilles. 1985 schedule includes Weber carburettor sets for Bristol engines, wiring looms, shock absorbers, valves, overriders for Ace, Aceca and Greyhound.

Sources for other items regularly listed in ACOC monthly magazine *Action*.

RP Engineering, 56 Hamm More Lane, Adlestone, Weybridge, Surrey.
Hub and wheel resplining and recutting.

BG Developments, 58 Sherwood Road, Aston Field Industrial Estate, Bromsgrove, Worcs.
Brake cylinder sleeving, recasting drums, etc.

CJ Engineering, 68A Lower City Road, Oldbury, Warley, West Midlands.
AC and Bristol engines, rebuilding, machining and race preparation.

Bristol Cars, Chiswick Flyover, Great West Road, London W4.
Bristol engines – most components, service and maintenance.

Paul Burd, 37 Arlington Road, St Annes, Bristol.
Bristol engines, secondhand and rebuilt parts, rebuilds and service.

Cobra

US-sourced parts:

John Woolf Racing, Woolf House, Norse Road, Bedford.
Imports Shelby American parts.

Shelby/Tiger/Cobra Parts and Restoration, 3099 Carter Drive, Kennesaw, GA 30144, USA.

CP Autokraft, Brooklands Industrial Park, Weybridge, Surrey.

UK-sourced parts:

Nick Green, 19 Chancellor House, Hyde Park Gate, London SW7.
Rebuilds and service.

B and D Racing Enterprise (chassis structures for Ace, Cobra Mk II). UK: The Old Manse, Kirkton of Prenmay, Nr Insch, Aberdeenshire. USA: Don Davis, 221 Jackson Street, Los Gatos, CA 95030, USA.

Two-Litre

See AC Cars and ACOC Spares Co-ordinator above.

APPENDIX A
Technical specifications

Two Litre 1947-1958
Engine: AC-built UMB series 6-cylinder 65 × 100mm, 1,991cc. CR 6.5:1 (1951 6.75 or 7:1). Triple SU Carbs, single overhead, chain-driven camshaft. 74bhp at 4,500rpm (1951 85bhp). Maximum torque 105lb ft at 2,750rpm. Cylinder head cast-iron, Aluminium-alloy crankcase and sump. Wet cylinder liners. Five main bearings (white-metal bearings until 1954, when engines followed Ace programme).
Transmission: Four-speed Moss gearbox with synchromesh on upper ratios. ENV final drive with 4.55:1 ratio. Overall gear ratios: 4.625:1, 6.32:1 9.16:1, 15.6:1 (1947); 4.55:1, 6.22:1, 9.01:1, 15.42:1 (1952). Gearing 17.8mph per 1,000rpm in top (1947), 18.0mph per 1,000rpm (1952).
Suspension and brakes: Beam axles and half elliptic leaf springs all round. 1947, Woodhead-Monroe telescopic dampers at front, Girling piston at rear; 1951 telescopics all round. Brakes 1947 Girling Hydro-mechanical, 1951 all hydraulic. Tyres 1947 5.00 – 17in later 6.70 – 16in. Worm-and-sector steering. Steel disc bolt-on wheels; 1953 centrelock wire wheels optional.
Dimensions: Wheelbase 9ft 9in; front track 4ft 7in; rear track 4ft 8in. Length 15ft 4in; width 5ft 7in; height 5ft 1in. Fuel tank 11½ gallons. Unladen weight 2,800lb (Buckland tourer 2,688lb).
Basic price: 1947 £1,000; 1949 £987; 1952 £1,214; Buckland £1,254.

Ace and Aceca 1953-1962
Engines: AC engine: construction as Two Litre UMB 1953. 1954 UMC CR 7.5:1, 85bhp at 4,500rpm, maximum torque 105lb/ft at 2,750rpm. 1955 (chassis AE505) CL series with steel-backed lead-indium bronze main, steel-backed lead-bronze connecting rod bearings, improved lubrication, 90bhp at 4,500rpm, CR 8:1, torque 110lb/ft at 2,500rpm. 1958 CLB series CR 9:1, 102bhp at 5,000rpm, later CLBN series with nitrided crankshaft.
Bristol: 6-cylinder, 66 × 96mm 1,971cc. CR:100B 8.5:1, 100D 8.5:1, 100D2 9.0:1. Triple Solex carburettors, pushrod overhead valve gear. Cast-iron crankcase, light-alloy head. Four main bearings. 100B 105bhp at 4,750rpm, maximum torque 123lb/ft at 3,750rpm; 100D 120bhp at 6,000rpm, maximum torque 120lb/ft at 4,250rpm; 100D2 125bhp at 6,000rpm, maximum torque 122lb/ft at 4,500rpm, later 130bhp at 5,750rpm, maximum torque 128lb/ft at 4,500rpm.
Ford 2.6: 6-cylinder 82.5 × 79.5mm 2,553cc. 90bhp at 4,400rpm, maximum torque 133lb/ft at 2,000rpm (see below for tuning stages).

Cast-iron block and head, pushrod overhead valves. Tuning stages: St 1 Ford head, 90bhp at 5,000rpm; St 2 adds larger valves, polished ports, triple SU carb, lightweight pistons, 125 at 5,500rpm; St 3 adds light-alloy six-port head, 130bhp at 5,000rpm; St 4 adds light pistons, 150bhp at 5,500rpm; St 5 adds Weber carburettors and alloy pushrods, 170bhp at 5,800rpm.
Transmission: ENV hypoid-bevel final-drive with 3.37, 3.64, 3.96, 4.3, 4.55, 4.88 or 5.11 ratios. Four-speed gearbox, ratios 1954, 3.64:1, final-drive 4.98:1, 7.21:1, 12.34:1. Aceca 1955, 3.96:1, 5.43:1, 7.85:1, 13.5:1. Ace-Bristol 1958, 3.91:1, 5.06:1, 7.03:1, 11.42:1. Gearing: 1954 Ace, 21.4mph per 1,000rpm; Aceca 1956, 19.5mph per 1,000rpm, Ace-Bristol 1958, 20.18mph per 1,000rpm. Overdrive gearing, 1956 Aceca: 3.2:1, 3.91:1, 4.38:1, 6.35:1, 7.85:1, 13.5:1; 25mph per 1,000rpm in overdrive.
Suspension and brakes: Fully independent, transverse leaf spring upper link, wishbone lower front and rear. Telescopic dampers. Extra leaf and heavy duty dampers at front 2.6 versions. Brakes: 11in by 1¾in drum 2LS at front, 1956, 11⅝in discs at front. Tyres: 5.50 – 16 braced tread or crossply. Centrelock wire wheels.
Dimensions: Wheelbase 7ft 6in; front and rear track 4ft 2in; length 12ft 8½in (Aceca 13ft 4in); width 4ft 11in (Aceca 5ft 1in); height 4ft 1in (Aceca 5ft 1in), Fuel tank 13 gallons. Weight 1,685lb (Aceca 1,840lb).
Basic price: 1954 Ace, £1,015; 1958 Ace-Bristol, £1,443; 1961, St 4 2.6 £1,197; Aceca 1955, £1,215; Aceca-Bristol 1960, £1,700.

Greyhound 1959-1962
Engines: As Ace/Aceca except Bristol 110 Series: 68.7 × 84.5mm, 2,216cc, CR 8.5:1, 105bhp at 4,700rpm, maximum torque 129lb/ft at 3,000rpm.
Transmission: 110 Series: 4.1:1 overall ratio. With overdrive, 3.2:1, 4.1:1, 5.24:1, 7.44:1, 11.92:1. 18.5mph per 1,000rpm; 23.7mph per 1,000rpm in O/D.
Suspension and brakes: Front, independent by wishbone and coil spring, rear independent by semi-trailing arms and coil springs. Brakes: 11¾in discs at front, 11in × 1¼in drums at rear. Steering gear: rack-and-pinion. Tyres: 6.40 – 15 crossply or 5.50 – 16 braced tread. Centre-lock wire wheels.
Dimensions: Wheelbase 8ft 4in; track 4ft 6¼in. Length 15ft 0in, height 4ft 4¾in, width 5ft 5¼in. Weight 2,240lb. Fuel tank 14 gallons.
Basic price: Bristol engine, with overdrive, £2,182.

Cobra 260 Mk I, 289 Mk II

Engine: Cobra 260: V8 3.8 × 2.87in (96.5 × 72.9mm), 260cid (4,261cc). CR 9.2:1, single 4-choke carburettor, solid valve lifters, pushrod operated overhead valves. Five main bearings. 260bhp at 5,800rpm, maximum torque 269ft/lb at 4,500rpm.

Cobra 289 4.0 × 2.87in (101.6 × 72.9mm), 289cid (4,735cc). CR 11.0:1. Single 4-choke carburettor, 300bhp at 5,750rpm, maximum torque 285lb/ft at 4,500rpm. Tuning stages for 289 motor: Stock Ford, 271bhp; porting and polishing heads, 298bhp; high-rise manifold with large-capacity 4-choke carburettor, 316bhp; steel shim head gaskets, 329bhp mill head to CR 11.6:1, 338bhp; free-flow exhaust system, 355bhp. Full-race engine Magnafluxed, balanced, crankshaft reworked, pistons modified, ports cleaned up and polished, larger valves, special camshaft, degreed crankshaft damper, reworked distributor, large capacity steel racing sump, twin 4-throat carburettors on high-rise manifold, 370/400bhp at 6,500/7,000rpm.

Suspension and brakes: As Ace, much reworking in detail. Mk I, worm-and-sector steering; Mk II rack-and-pinion. Brakes: disc all round, front 11.7in diam, rear 10.75in diam. Tyres Mk I 6.50 – 15 front, 6.70 – 15 rear. Mk II street, 185 – 15. Limited-slip differential.

Transmission: Mk I, final-drive ratio 3.54:1. All-synchromesh four-speed manual box, overall ratios 3.54:1, 4.99:1, 6.30:1, 8.36:1. Street Mk II, 3.77:1, 5.29:1, 6.71:1, 8.89:1. Final-drive ratios available, 1964: 2.72, 3.31, 3.54, 3.77, 4.26, 4.56:1. Cast-magnesium pin-drive centrelock wheels up to 8½ – 15in, optional 72-spoke wire wheels.

Dimensions: Wheelbase 7ft 6in; front track 4ft 5½in; rear track 4ft 5¾in. Length 13ft 2in, width 5ft 3in; height 4ft. Unladen weight 2,100lb, fuel tank 18 gallons.

Basic price: £2,260 (Mk II).

Cobra 427 Mk III, AC 289 Mk III

Engines: Cobra 427: V8, 4.24 × 3.78in (107 × 96mm) 427 cid (6,998cc) CR 10.4:1, twin 4-choke carburettors, solid valve lifters pushrod operated inclined valves. Cast-iron block, aluminium cylinder heads, five main bearings. 480bhp at 6,000rpm, 480ft/lb at 3,700rpm.

428 engine: 4.14in. × 3.98in (104.9 × 101.2mm) 428cid, (7,014cc). Cast-iron head and block. CR 10.5:1. Single 4-choke carburettor. 345bhp at 4,600rpm, maximum torque 462lb/ft at 2,800rpm.

428 modified by Shelby American 390bhp at 5,200rpm, maximum torque 475ft/lb at 3,700rpm. Mechanical valve lifters. Tuning stages: 427 engines available with modified lubrication system (side-oilers), low-, medium-, high-riser inlet manifolds, forged-steel crankshafts, CR to 11.6:1/14.0:1, special long-dwell and high-lift camshafts, etc, to 600bhp at 8,500rpm.

289: refer to 289 Mk II specification.

Transmission: 427 overall ratio 3.54:1, 4.57, 5.98, 8.21:1. Optional final-drive ratio include 3.77, 3.09, 3.31, 4.09:1. All-synchromesh manual four speed box, limited slip differential. Close ratio gears also available.

Suspension and brakes: Anti-dive, anti-squat suspension front and rear using unequal-length wishbones all round with semi-trailing arms at rear. Coil springs. Disc brakes, 11.63in diam front,, 10.75in diam rear. Tyres up to 11.40-15 on cast magnesium-alloy pin drive wheels with centrelock hubs up to 9.5-15. 289 Mk III tyres: 185-15 on 6½L-15 72-spoke wire wheels.

Dimensions: Wheelbase 7ft 6in; front track 4ft 6¼in; rear track 4ft 6in. Length 13ft 3in, width 5ft 5in. Fuel tank (street) 15 gallons. Dry weight 2,354lb.

Basic price: 427, USA $7,000, 289; Mk III, £2,400.

AC428 Frua 1965-1973

Engine: 428 as Cobra Mk III, 428 engine

Transmission: Ford G6 automatic three-speed with torque coverter. Overall ratio 2.88:1. Top 1.0-2.0, inter 1.46-2.92, low 2.46-4.36. 29.8mph per 1,000rpm. Limited-slip differential.

Suspension and brakes: As Cobra Mk III but not adjustable suspension. Tyres 205-15, wheels 6-15. 72-spoke wire centrelock wheels.

Dimensions: Wheelbase, 7ft 11¾in, front track 4ft 5¼in, rear track 4ft 6½in. Length 14ft 8¼in; height 4ft 1½in, width 5ft 8½in. Fuel tank 18 gallons. Unladen weight 3,155lb.

Basic price £4,245.

AC Mk IV

Engine: Ford 'Windsor' V8, cast-iron, to full Federal Emission Control specification. 4,948cc (302cid). Single Holley carb. 212bhp net (Europe 230bhp net). Ford Motorsport equipment to owner's choice takes power to 450/500bhp net.

Transmission: Borg-Warner T5 (MX335) 5-speed gearbox, all-synchro. Ratios 3.35:1, 1.93:1, 1.29:1, 1:1 and 0.68:1. Rear axle: Salisbury limited-slip, 3.35:1.

Suspension and brakes: Independent suspension by unequal-length wishbones and concentric coil springs and dampers front and rear. Four-wheel disc brakes, 11.63in vented front, 10.75in rear. Two independent servo-assisted circuits. Wheels and tyres: Halibrand-pattern aluminium-alloy peg-drive, 7 × 16in front, 8 × 16in rear. Goodyear Eagle GT steel-braced radial tyres, 225/50 VR16 front, 255/50 VR16 rear.

Dimensions: Weight 2,620lb, wheelbase 90in, front track 56in, rear track 60in; length 162in, width 68in, height 49in. Fuel capacity 15 Imperial gallons.

APPENDIX B
Chassis number sequences and production figures

With a specialist car made in small numbers, it is often difficult to identify exactly which were made at any given period. Factory prototypes, demonstrators, cars provided for a director's personal use, even vehicles returned unsold from a distributor, will re-appear on the factory's books and be accounted for sometimes out of sequence. In AC's case the fat ledgers in which are listed all the cars they have built since 1930 contain a preliminary column headed 'Date to Distributor'. It follows that in arriving at annual production figures, the number of cars passed to a distributor will not necessarily agree precisely with the sequence of chassis numbers allocated during that same period. In this summary I have followed the practice of counting in any calendar year every car or chassis released from the factory during that 12-month period, even though it may be evident that it was actually made anything from six months to several years earlier.

When production began once again after the Second World War, AC Cars were able to break free of the model-year policy they had followed before 1940. Modifications – even as important as the adoption of the Bristol engine – were introduced with little publicity; the cars were changed little in styling and equipment while they remained in production. As far as possible, the first and last cars built in any year are recorded.

1946 to 1958
Two Litre saloon, drophead, Buckland sports tourer.

Chassis continued with the L prefix, engines with the UMB prefix used pre-war. In 1949 substitution of ENV-built rear axles for those previously built by Moss Gear Co was marked by an EL prefix. When, in late 1951, hydraulic brakes were used all round, the prefix EH was adopted. Export left-hand-drive cars were given X at the end of the prefix. On engines, a W suffix indicated Wellworthy pistons to replace Specialloid. After the introduction of the Ace in 1954 the remaining saloons followed the engine numbering sequence of the new model.

1946

		Chassis	Engines	
6.4.46	Experimental drophead coupe	L800	UMB800	1

1947

3.1.47	Prototype saloon	L801		
	Production Two Litre saloon	L802		
		L815		16

1948

		Chassis	Engines	
31.2.48	Two Litre saloon	L805		
12.1.48	Two Litre saloon	L816		1
24.12.48	Two Litre saloon	L1017		201
				202

(Chassis nos. L806 to 815 not allocated)

1948

3.1.49	Two Litre saloon	L1018		
30.12.49	Two Litre saloon	EL1291	UMB1292	273
8.12.49	Two Litre saloon	L1295		1
5.12.49	Chassis only	L1303		1
				275

(Chassis nos. 1292, 1293, 1294 not allocated)

1950

5.1.50	Two Litre saloon	EL1292		
13.11.50	Two Litre saloon	EL1557		
				267

(Chassis nos. 1437, 1295, 1303 not allocated; add Chassis nos. 1564, 1573, 1580)

1951

3.1.51	Two Litre saloon	EL1558		
?.12.51	Two Litre saloon	EH1844		
				278

(Chassis nos. 1564, 1573, 1580 to 1950.
Chassis nos. 1824, 1835, 1836, 1840, 1843 to 1952)

1952-53

8.2.52	Two Litre saloon	EH1845	UMB1847W	
25.11.53	Buckland tourer	EH2051	UMB2045W	
				204

(Chassis nos. 2045, 2046* not allocated)

1954-55

28.2.54	Two Litre saloon	EH2052	UMB2061W	
25.10.55	Two Litre saloon	EH2086	CL2186W	34
22.12.55	Two Litre saloon	EH2089	CL2216W	1
				35

1956-58

22.9.56	Two Litre saloon 4 Door	EH2087	CL2201	
1.1.57	Two Litre saloon 4 Door	EH2093		
	(Chassis nos. 2089, 2090 not allocated)			5

		Chassis	Engines	
14.2.58	Two Litre saloon 2 Door	EH2094		1
16.5.58	Two Litre saloon 2 Door	EH2095		1
				7

Note: *Chassis no. 2046 appears in the current ACOC Register.

1954 to 1964
Ace roadster and Aceca GT coupe.

It is evident from the AC records that during the production life of the Ace and Aceca, cars initially built up with AC engines could be re-engined with Bristol units before delivery. These cars were renumbered from the AE (AC engine) series to the BE (Bristol engine). The first AC-engined Ace was AE01 but production started at AE22. AC-engined Aceca production started with AEC56, converted from an Ace, then began in earnest with AE499. The first Ace-Bristol was BE109 (ex AE109) and Bristol-engined Aces generally were numbered in the same sequence as the AC-engined Aces. The first Aceca-Bristol was BE570. The Ace 2.6 sequence began with RS5000, the Aceca 2.6 was numbered from RS5500. Export left-hand-drive vehicles were identified by a final X on the prefix.

In the summary given below the annual totals are taken directly from the AC Cars records. Ace chassis numbers quoted for each year give the first and last built as far as can be determined. The Aceca number quoted is the last one built in each year, as far as can be determined. The original Tojeiro-Ace chassis is not numbered.

1954

		Chassis	Engines	Aceca	Ace
14.5.54	Ace	AE22	UMB2043		
19.11.54	Ace	AEX54	UMB2115		22
8.10.54	Aceca	AEC56(1)			1
					23

1955

		Chassis	Engines	Aceca	Ace
21.1.55	Ace	AE37	UMB2089		
8.3.57	Ace	AE42	UMB1914		
1.3.58	Ace	AE(BE)109			62
	Aceca	AE536	CL2212	50	
					112

1956

		Chassis	Engines	Aceca	Ace
14.2.56	Ace	AEX98	CL2203W		
27.12.56	Ace	BEX242	100D558		110
	Aceca	AEX594		40	
					150

1957

		Chassis	Engines	Aceca	Ace
15.4.57	Ace	AEX163	CL2297		
20.12.57	Ace	BEX394	100D748		176
30.11.57	Aceca	BEX640	100D747	49	
					225

1958

		Chassis	Engines	Aceca	Ace
3.5.58	Ace	BE367	100D714		
22.12.58	Ace	BEX1040	100D2718		104
	Aceca	BE717		84	
					188

1959

		Chassis	Engines	Aceca	Ace
1.5.59	Ace	BE497	100D2876		
14.12.59	Ace	BEX1122	100D2980		104
	Aceca	BEX765		48	
					112

1960

		Chassis	Engines	Greyhound	Aceca	Ace
8.3.60	Ace	AEX1106	CLB2433			
16.12.60	Ace	AEX119	CLBN2477WT			63
14.9.60	Aceca	BE812	100B2 3834		44	
1959-60						
	Greyhound	BEF2500	100D2 1164	17		
		BEF2517				
						124

1961

		Chassis	Engines	Greyhound	Aceca	Ace
23.10.61	Ace	BEX1169	100D2 1070			
8.12.61	Ace	BEX1205	100D2 1170			10
	Aceca	AE821			8	
	Greyhound	BEF2516	110 5180			
		BEF2563	100D2 1154	44		
	Aceca 2.6	RSX5500			3	
	Ace 2.6	RS5000				8
						73

1962

		Chassis	Engines	Greyhound	Aceca	Ace
11.1.62	Ace	BEX1199	100D2 1080			
3.10.62	Ace	BEX1211	100D2 1162			3
19.10.62	Aceca	BE819	100D2 1141		8	
	Greyhound	BEF2557	110D2 1142			
		BEF2582		18		
	Aceca 2.6	RSX5503			5	
	Ace 2.6	RS5026				20
						54

1963

		Chassis	Engines	Greyhound	Aceca	Ace
5.10.63	Ace	AE1190	CLBN2474WT			
19.4.63	Ace	BE1218	100D2 1177			9
	Aceca	A83		1		
	Greyhound	BEF2553	100D2 1126			
		BEF2578	100D2 1162	3		
	Aceca 2.6	RS5036			10	
						23

1964

		Chassis	Engines	Greyhound	Aceca	Ace
21.3.64	Ace	BEX1186				
26.3.64	Ace	BEX1187	100D2 1078			2
						2

1962 to 1973

Shelby American AC Cobra, AC 289 roadsters, AC 428 convertibles and fastback coupes.

1962			Cobra Euro	Cobra USA & total
20.2.62	CSX 2000	Airfreighted New York unpainted		
19.7.62	CSX 2001	Airfreighted New		
24.7.62	CSX 2002	Airfreighted Los Angeles		
27.7.62	CSX 2003	Seafreighted New York		
31.7.62	CSX 2004	Seafreighted New York		
	CS 2030	AC Cars demonstrator		
12.12.62	CSX 2060			61
1963				
1.1.63	CSX 2061			
5.4.63	CS 2130			
10.12.63	CSX 2259	First car of 1963-64 homologation series		
30.12.63	CSX 2276			215
1.10.63	COB 6001			
13.11.63	COB 6004		5	
	COB 6005	Ex-prototype sold 1965	1	
				221
1964				
6.1.64	CSX 2277			
20.1.64	CSX 2301	Race car. Wide rear wings, despatched in primer		
25.10.64	CSX 2702	Last of this series as CSX 2301		425

1964			Cobra Euro	Cobra USA & total
4.3.64	COB 6006	Mk2		
29.12.64	COB 6049	Mk2	39	
23.10.64	CSX 3001	Mk3	Unpainted	
23.10.64	CSX 3002	Mk3	Unpainted	2
				465
1965				
1.1.65	CSX 3003	Mk3	Unpainted	
24.3.65	CSX 3055	Mk3	Unpainted	54
2.4.65	CSX 3101	Mk3		
24.11.65	CSX 3201	Mk3		200
19.1.65	COB 6027	Mk2		
3.5.65	COB 6062	Mk2		14
				214
1966				
10.1.66	CSX 3202	Mk3		
28.12.66	CSX 3358	Mk3		157

			Cobra Euro	Cobra USA & total
27.4.66	COB 6101	Mk3		
25.11.66	CSX 6112	Mk3	12	
15.8.69	CF 1	428		
	CF 3		3	
				172
1967				
19.5.67	COB 6114	Mk3		
	COB 6120	Mk3	7	
28.11.67	CFX 4			
	CF 5		2	
				9
1968				
13.6.68	COB 6121	Mk3		
	COB 6132	Mk3	10	
1.3.68	CF 6	428		
21.11.68	CF 23	428	17	
				27
1969				
5.6.69	MX 1	Chassis only	1	
17.1.69	CF 24	428		
5.11.69	CF 46	428	21	
	EFX 501	(Electric Traction)		8
	EXX 508	"		30
1970				
5.1.70	CF 47			
	CF 59		11	
24.10.70	EX 509		1	
				12
1971				
6.9.71	CF 53			
23.6.71	CF 64		7	
				7
1972				
13.10.72	CF 66			
	CF 79		13	
				13
1973				
10.1.73	CF 65			
	CF 80		3	
				3

APPENDIX C
How fast? How economical? How heavy?
Performance figures for postwar AC models

I have confined my summary to results originally published in the British weekly journals *Autocar* and *Motor*. *Autocar* have always used the fifth-wheel device, *Motor* changed from stopwatches to fifth-wheel along the way. The different methods may result in the times they recorded varying, but they are very minor differences. Kerb weight usually included some 5 gallons of fuel and both journals measured performance with a full passenger load; thus the 428 for example, was tested with about 450lb more than its kerb weight. Other journals were less exacting. John Bolster's tests for *Autosport* were usually carried out with only the driver on board. His figures tend to be rather higher than other testers'. The American journals *Road & Track* and *Car and Driver* did carry out fully-loaded tests. They both quoted a 427 at 2,890lb against the kerb weight of 2,529lb.

Two Litre to Greyhound
Although as a revised prewar design the Two Litre could not compete with good specimens of postwar practice such as the lively Jowett Javelin, it matched more traditional competitors on test. These are 1953 figures:

	0-50mph	standing ¼-mile
AC Two Litre	14.5sec	22.2sec
Vanguard Ph II 2 litre	13.6sec	21.6sec
Daimler Conquest 2½ litre	16.3sec	23.2sec
Citroen Big 15 2 litre	16.4sec	23.7sec

I believe the best figures for an Ace were published in Dennis May's article on an Ace 2.6, for *Car and Driver* in 1961. He recorded 0-50mph in 6sec, the standing quarter-mile in 16.2sec and a maximum of 130mph, possibly with the hood erect. In the same year, *Motor Sport* did 123.8mph, 0-50mph in 7.5sec, 0-60mph in 10.0sec, with a standing quarter-mile in 16.8sec. This 2.6 car was in Stage 4 tune. John Bolster claimed a hand-timed 15.6sec for a standing quarter-mile with a 2.6. 700 BBP, put into st 4 tune by Rudd before passing it to the works. Another similar Ace has been timed electronically in club events at 16.1sec.

Perhaps the most provocative test of an AC Aceca was John Bolster's 1959 outing in a 128bhp 100D2-engined version. He managed to work up to 128.57mph top speed, the standing quarter-mile in 16.6sec, 0-50mph in 6.4sec and 0-60mph in 9.4sec. Driven hard, the Aceca recorded 22.5mpg.

Cobra
Roger Bell's figures for *Motor* really say it all. But there are a number of interesting performances in addition. Bolster did a standing quarter-mile in 13.8sec on a damp road, using Shelby's early Mk II in 1963. *Car and Driver* did a standing quarter-mile in 12.2sec in 1965 and managed the 0-100mph-0 cycle in 14.5sec, all with a Mk III 427 and without special techniques. Shelby works driver Ken Miles is reputably reported to have done the same in 13.8sec. Roger Bell's figures in 1967 with the ex-John Woolfe 427, possibly the car campaigned in European classic races by Freutel and Settembre, were to leave it as the fastest accelerating car tested by *Motor* for many years.

continued overleaf

	Two-Litre saloon	Ace 1991cc	Aceca 1991cc	Ace-Bristol 100D2	Aceca-Bristol 100D2	Ace 2.6 (St 4)	Greyhound 100D2	Cobra 289 Mk II	Cobra 427 Mk III	AC 289 Mk III	AC 428 Frua Auto
Mean maximum speed (mph)	77.0	103.0	102.0	117.0	115.5	112.5	104.3	138.0	165.0	134.9	139.3
Acceleration (sec)											
0-30mph	6.3	3.9	4.4	3.5	4.0	2.3	4.3	1.5	1.8	2.5	2.2
0-40mph	–	5.9	–	4.7	5.9	4.7	6.4	2.5	2.6	3.4	3.3
0-50mph	14.4	7.9	9.7	6.8	8.0	6.5	8.9	4.0	3.4	4.4	4.6
0-60mph	21.0	11.4	13.4	9.1	10.3	8.1	11.4	5.5	4.2	5.6	5.9
0-70mph	–	15.1	19.4	12.4	14.1	11.5	16.7	7.0	5.7	7.2	7.7
0-80mph	–	20.1	25.7	15.8	18.2	14.4	21.1	8.0	6.8	9.0	9.6
0-90mph	–	28.9	37.2	19.9	23.7	17.8	27.0	11.0	8.5	11.3	11.8
0-100mph	–	–	–	27.0	33.1	23.3	37.6	13.0	10.3	13.7	14.5
0-110mph	–	–	–	40.4	–	36.2	–	17.0	13.1	17.9	19.0
0-120mph	–	–	–	–	–	–	–	18.0	16.4	22.8	–
Standing ¼-mile (sec)	22.2	18.0	19.1	16.5	17.8	16.6	18.9	13.9	12.4	14.4	14.4
Direct top gear (sec)											
10-30mph	16.2	8.8	–	–	–	6.3	9.4	–	–	–	–
20-40mph	14.9	8.8	–	–	10.2	5.8	9.9	–	3.2	3.9	–
30-50mph	15.8	9.2	9.7	8.9	10.0	5.9	10.6	–	3.4	4.2	–
40-60mph	18.2	9.4	9.5	8.7	10.3	6.0	11.0	–	3.6	4.2	–
50-70mph	–	9.9	10.8	8.5	11.3	6.3	13.0	–	3.9	4.3	–
60-80mph	–	11.6	–	8.6	11.5	6.3	13.0	–	4.1	4.1	–
70-90mph	–	15.2	–	7.3	12.7	6.8	13.9	–	4.1	4.7	
80-100mph	–	–	–	12.6	15.4	9.1	18.6	–	–	5.0	–
90-110mph	–	–	–	19.7	–	–	–	–	–	6.1	–
100-120mph	–	–	–	–	–	–	–	–	–	8.0	–
Overall fuel consumption (mpg)	19.1	25.2	20.5	21.6	20.5	21.1	19.9	15.1	–	15.2	16.4
Typical fuel consumption (mpg)	–	–	–	–	–	–	21.8	–	11/15	16.3	16.6
Kerb weight (lb)	2912	1685	2156	1845	2184	1929	2410	2315	2529	2352	3220
Test published (**Motor, rest Autocar)	1953	1954**	1956	1958	1960	1961**	1961**	1965	1967**	1967**	1968